Feeling Happy And Making Happy

By

Allen Shaw

ISBN: 1469936011
ISBN 13: 9781469936017

To Joel, Lucy, Louis and Alex

Contents

Introduction v

Part 1: Happiness for All 1

1. What is happiness? 3

2. How do we find happiness? 13

3. Why happiness is the ultimate good 33

4. Growing old and staying happy 47

5. Feeling more peaceful about dying. 65

6. Justice between the generations 81

7. Why does making other people happy make us
    happy? 95

8. Our happiness or their happiness?. 111

9. Reasons to care about the happiness
    of others. 125

10. Should we really care about the
    happiness of others? 141

11. How should we go about making others happy?. . 159

12. Religious duty or general happiness? 175

Part II: Feeling Happier About Tough Moral Decisions 193

13. Tackling decisions 195

14.   Making decisions 209
15.   When is it right to kill innocent animals? 223
16.   Can it be right to kill an innocent human? 239

Conclusion 259
References and notes 261

Introduction

We all want to be happy and a great way to be happy is to make other people happy. This book is about feeling happy and making others happy, especially as we grow older because so many of us are older.

It starts with a look at what happiness is and why we have a duty to try to achieve it without a right to have everything that we might want. It is the supreme good for us and for others. Fortunately making others happy usually does the same for us. I go on to discuss more directly what to do to be happy and then specifically how to stay that way, as we age and face death. We also have to consider a fair balance between the happiness of one generation and that of the next.

There are reasons which make most of us care about others, but sometimes we have to choose between their happiness and ours. Why should we care about others, if their happiness gives us no pleasure? Duty to God is one reason to care for them. Or we can just accept that a duty to care for others is fundamental and requires no reason. All arguments which deny that duty are flawed.

There are moral principles which guide us in our approach to others but they do not bind us totally. Religion is based on following right principles and utilitarianism is based on achieving good goals. Both are important guides to our treatment of others but our heads and our hearts tell us that sometimes either of them can be wrong.

Moral doubts and disagreements cause unhappiness and I describe a four step process to use when in those situations. It looks systematically first at the facts of a situation and then the consequences of possible actions. Then it assembles the principles underlying each possible action and finally it looks at how to choose between the actions suggested by the different principles. I apply the process to eating meat, benefiting from animal experiments, mercy killing and abortion. It gives answers which will satisfy no extreme view.

My main concern is with what we should do as individuals, not with what society should do or what the law should be. I draw on the great philosophers, steering clear of all jargon, and also on the wisdom of religion but with a critical eye. It still influences us. We may discard the belief, but it is neither possible nor desirable to discard most of the ethic. The boy may leave religion but religion will not leave the boy.

My first qualification for writing came without effort. I just grew older. My second came at cost. I spent my working life looking after people at their best and their worst, at their happiest and most miserable. My job was to make them healthier and therefore happier. I was paid to do it but seeing them happier made me happier.

I started as a hospital porter, became a consultant physician and finished as a clinical assistant. Chairing a medical ethics committee led me to look into moral philosophy and religion. I started to think about my happiness and the happiness of other people. I stopped publishing clinical research papers and started writing on ethics. It seemed that happiness was the supreme good for each of us and spreading it was the crux of morality. So I wrote this book.

From experience I know that it is easier to fail to be happy and fail to make others happy than it is to succeed. But those who find practice difficult, are well equipped to teach as I found when I taught my grandson to ride a bicycle, without ever mastering that simple art myself. Writing a book is different from setting an example.

Mixed success with patients, examiners, interviewers, journal editors and pretty girls has taught me valuable lessons. Never dwell on disappointments but go on to the next challenge. We flourish by hope and persistence, not regrets and remorse. Accept undeserved bad luck with resilience and undeserved good luck with enthusiasm.

For brevity male pronouns are meant to include both sexes without intending any sexism. Mankind includes womankind. God is awarded masculinity and this is balanced by ascribing femininity to doctors, although they have long lost any god-like pretensions.

Many have unwittingly helped me by teaching, example and discussion. Norma has shown immense patience during my affairs with word processors and worked hard to make my writing readable. Sue Lascelles and Stanley Shaw gave me useful advice and Lucy Barker helped to design the cover. I hope you find parts of the book useful and parts amusing.

PART I

Happiness for all

1

What Is Happiness?

All we can do is to be happy and do the best we can while we are still alive.

ECCLESIASTES III. 12

That quotation says three things. Happiness is the supreme good, so we are entitled to try hard to be happy. We also should do the best we can and presumably that means helping others to be happy. Third, there is no point bothering about what will happen after we are dead. We have this one life to do what we can.

So what is happiness? It is a state of mind but beyond that it is difficult to define. The dictionary and the thesaurus can only offer synonyms, which do not even mean quite the same as happiness. The neuroscientist may say that it is associated with activity in certain parts of the brain. Such activity may accompany happiness or even be the direct cause of it, which does not tell us what it is. But we do know that it is a state we want to be in and stay in. We are pleased that we are alive to enjoy it. We can also describe its features and the ways to achieve it.

We think that we will stay happy, at least for a long time, because if we thought our happiness was soon coming to an end, it would certainly put a damper on us. The condemned man does not enjoy his last breakfast as much as he would, if he were just going for a little walk afterwards.

Happy people have a good opinion of themselves. If they did not, they would not be happy. Sufferers from depressive illness think that they do not deserve to be happy and that is exactly what they are not. Guilt or regrets over some stupidity can also make us think that we do not deserve to be happy. Then we wish that we had not done whatever we did and still deserved to be happy. Fortunately our stupidity or our nastiness do not always cause as much trouble as they might have done. For that we can be grateful.

Happiness levels fluctuate. Sometimes there is a reason, as my wife found when she realised that it was my suitcase the airline lost, not her identical one. Sometimes levels fluctuate for no reason. Moods are more variable in some than others. You have an equable temperament but I have bouts of depression alternating with periods of pleasurable energy. In extreme cases it amounts to manic-depressive psychosis.

Both good and bad events affect our happiness levels. But in response a phenomenon called hedonic adaptation occurs.

After triumphs or disasters we tend to return to our default level of happiness. If you win the lottery, a year later you will be no happier than you were before. If you have spent the cash unwisely and lost your real friends because they could not keep up with you, you may be less happy than before your dream came true. Even the ecstasy of romantic love lasts only about six months, perhaps longer if it is unrequited. When love is satisfied our biochemistry returns to normal and love changes its nature or becomes disillusion.

However, events which cause a permanent change in our situation like chronic illness, bereavement, or unemployment do cause prolonged unhappiness. Our mood sets at a lower level, even though it still fluctuates. Long lasting pain, disability, financial worries or loss of social contacts inevitably have long lasting effects.

When we are happy negative emotions like anxiety, guilt, and anger are absent or much reduced. Envy is also reduced. You will be less happy, if you think that she is happier than you. Unpleasant physical sensations, such as pain, shortness of breath, hunger and thirst also reduce or destroy happiness. Finding a chopstick to scratch a persistent itch under a plaster provides a welcome increase in happiness.

Finally an important feature of happiness is its communicability, which is one reason why there is a duty to try to be happy.

The duty to be happy

The great philosopher Immanuel Kant (1724-1804) said that we should act in the way that we think that everyone should act. [1] It would seem reasonable to add that we should want to feel in the way we want everyone to feel. As I hope that you would want everyone to feel happy you ought to want to feel happy yourself.

If you believe in God, you should want his creatures to be happy and we are each one of God's creatures, so it is right to try to be happy yourself. After all you are his creature that you know best. You are the one, over whose actions you have the most influence. Also Kant gives another reason why we have a moral duty to try to be happy.

> To secure one's own happiness is a duty....for discontent with one's condition…. might easily become a great temptation to transgress one's duties. [2]

Happiness makes us nicer. If we come home happy from work, we do not even feel like kicking the dog. Happier people are overall more helpful than unhappy people. They want others to be happy and even go so far as to do something about it. So other people are happier and therefore nicer to us, which in turn makes us happier. Reinforcement comes from the interaction.

Immanuel Kant was probably the greatest modern philosopher. He was a bachelor of such settled habits that the citizens of Koenigsberg in Prussia set their clocks when he passed their houses on his daily stroll. Germany is noted particularly for its musicians, its philosophers and its previous propensity to invade other people's countries.

Happiness improves our health and lengthens our lives. It makes us more effective and increases our creativity and ability to solve problems. It improves our social skills and makes us more extroverted. These are primarily personal benefits but they also enable us to do more for others. The happy extrovert helps the rest of us without even trying. Shared laughter binds us together. Would you rather sit next to an introvert or an extrovert at dinner?

There is good evidence that our happiness spreads to others. The greater our contact with people and the nearer their geographic closeness to us, the greater is the effect. The emotional contagion spreads to spouses, siblings, friends and neighbours. [3] But it does not just spread to our friends; it spreads to our friends' friends' friends, of whose existence we are quite unaware. Fortunately that need not deter us from helping unhappy people, because it seems that their unhappiness does not contaminate us too much. [3]

Oxytocin (the cuddle hormone) makes us trusting, trustworthy, friendly and generous. When we exhibit these traits others produce more oxytocin and that makes them display the same qualities. What we do is mediated by chemicals and determined by heredity and upbringing but we still have powers of decision.

Happiness and goodness are contagious and that is one of the blessings granted to mankind along with our inability to foresee personal misfortune.

Is there a right to actually be happy?

I did not say that we have a right to be happy, only a right to try to be. So what are rights? When we speak of them we mean that something unpleasant should not happen to us or that something pleasant should. We are thinking of what other people should or should not do to us or for us. So we can only have a right when someone else has a duty to us.

There are negative rights, which everyone owes us, such as not to injure us or deprive us of liberty or property unjustly, all of which would reduce our happiness. As far as they go we do have a right to be happy. The rub comes of course with deciding what is just.

Then there are positive rights, which we think that no one should be denied, such as adequate food, clean water, and education. Certain political rights might be included here. We can probably all agree on some basic standards about these matters. The problem is to decide who has the duty to provide the right. Usually the rich are more interested in getting richer than in making the poor less poor. All of us, who have much more than basic needs, have some duty to help those who lack such essential requirements for happiness. People who govern have a more specific duty to the governed.

It is possible to be happy in the absence of those negative and basic positive rights but it hardly helps. There are two advantages to thinking in terms of rights, not just of duties. It helps to make us all uncomfortable that some lack basic negative and positive rights. It encourages the deprived actively to seek remedies from those who willfully fail to fulfil their duties to them.

There is a third type of right, which people in affluent countries think is essential to their happiness. It is a positive right to material luxuries. Seeing these luxuries as an entitlement and essential to happiness is counter-productive. It makes us discontented. It is also dangerous. It encourages individuals and nations to incur debts, which they cannot easily repay. That leads to unhappiness greater than the original discontent.

Our televisions encourage conspicuous consumption. People naturally think that they are entitled to a piece of what they see. Advertisements tell people to pay nothing for two years but do not add that they will then be in debt for something old, when they already want something else new. Then they are told to roll up all their separate debts into a single, never-ending debt with their home as a security. So they lose the home they do need for their happiness because of greed for what they did not need. Others will always have more than we do and happiness does not come from pursuing an ever-receding goal.

A friend arranged a large discount on a new, fancy television for a colleague. But he had to pay cash to get the discount. His colleague could not afford to do this and wanted the television instantly. So rather than save for it, he paid the full retail price and the interest on a hire purchase agreement. This was a perfectly intelligent man, holding down a responsible job.

We have no right to everything that we think will make us happy and what we crave will probably not make us happy.

The dark side of happiness

Too much happiness makes us careless, easily fooled and overconfident. Then we fall flat on our faces. Success and happiness do not come with a guarantee of permanence. Perhaps it is good for us when life sometimes takes us down a peg or two when we do not expect it. You think that they all came to hear your talk and then someone tells you that they were only filling the gap between the popular lecturer before you and the free tea after you. Learning the truth can also destroy happiness completely.

A friend works for the homeless at Christmas. A client told her his story. He was a joiner, and finished work early one day, so he went home, where he found his wife in bed with a neighbour. He beat him up and went to prison. He lost his wife, his job, and his home. [4]

The first moral of the story is that it is more important to telephone your spouse that you are coming home early than that you are coming home late. The second is that it is bad to be deceived, but worse to be undeceived. The fool's paradise is a happy place, from which we may never be evicted. The joiner would still be happy, if he had not come home early.

When I was a very young house officer the surgeon removed an inflamed appendix. In that particular instance it might have been better to insert an abdominal drain. Possibly because of this omission an abscess developed and the man spent three months in hospital. He left with profuse thanks and presents all round. I still have his pewter pot. Perhaps my anxious face peering round the curtains at all hours showed him how concerned we all were about him. I wonder whether he would have been a happier man, if he had known that he might have been a victim of a mistake.

We enjoy gossiping about the faults and failures of our acquaintances more than we like talking about their virtues and successes. Even other people's misfortune can gladden the hearts of the best of us. The Germans call it "Schadenfreude". When it is envy of the tall trees then it is unworthy and suggests that we are unhappy. It is fine when we rejoice to see the arrogant get their come-uppance, a proportionate punishment for wrong done. It makes us feel that there is a little more justice in the world. It is even better when we see those, who were careless of our own feelings, get what was coming to them. But grim satisfaction struggles with concern when our children meet the same problems with their children, which drove us to despair with them.

We do meet people who seem to enjoy being gloomy. There are a few explanations for this. They may have a perverse satisfaction in explaining their low mood as the result of unfair treatment by others. They may feel martyred by a world that has singled them out for bad luck and misfortune. And just as we enjoy being happy with others we like to feel that others accompany us in our misery.

Finally common experience tells us that duty often conflicts with pleasure and sometimes we have to choose between the two.

2

How Do We Find Happiness?

The bad news is that our happiness level is half pre-set by our genes before we are born, so we can't do much about it. The good news is that half is not and we can do a lot about it. And by good luck we tend to be more optimistic than experience justifies. Half of marriages in the UK end in divorce but few newlyweds think it will happen to them.

Studies on twins separated at birth show that inheritance strongly influences us physically and mentally. Life insurers want to know how long your parents lived. If we are lucky, we are naturally agreeable, optimistic, emotionally stable extroverts open to new ideas and experiences. If we are also conscientious, that makes others lucky too. If we are unlucky, we are introverted, antagonistic, suspicious, neurotic pessimists with closed minds. And that is also bad luck for the people, who come our way. But we can be aware of and work on our less pleasant character traits. The way you play your cards can compensate for the poor hand you are dealt.

Happiness comes to us in different ways. One woman rejoices in mothering her children. Another finds a day spent with toddlers drives her spare. The old man loves his work and his younger brother joyfully embraces retirement. A few find happiness, not from personal fulfilment, but from caring for a cause outside themselves.

There are two main roads to happiness and we have to travel both simultaneously, a geographic but not a behavioural impossibility. We must act to stop ourselves being unhappy and we must also act to make ourselves happy.

NOT MAKING OURSELVES UNHAPPY

Misfortunes happen to most of us and they do make us unhappy. Marcus Aurelius (121-180), the stoic philosopher, tried to persuade himself that they should not, because they do not lessen our virtue. Tell that to a mother who has just lost her child. I doubt that a true stoic has ever walked this earth. All we can do is to endure and eventually find other consolations. But Marcus was right that it helps to feel that we do not need to add guilt to our sorrow. Life is a series of phases, long and short, good and bad. Do not worry about the good times ending and keep in mind that the bad ones usually do. We should not worry that happiness will not last but comfort ourselves that unhappiness does not.

Marcus Aurelius was a Roman emperor, the only emperor ever to be better known as a philosopher. He expressed his gratitude to his wife in his *Meditations* and promoted several of her lovers to posts of honour and profit. While he was away at the war she kept her home fire burning. He was the only man in his empire, who did not know what she was up to. The husband is always the last to know. And philosophers talk the talk better than they walk the walk.

Negative emotions blight our happiness. Guilt is inwardly directed; envy, anger and resentment are directed at other people; anxiety can float freely inside us or have an external focus.

Guilt is a useless emotion, although regret is necessary. If we have done something foolish or wrong, we should recognise it and work out why we did it so that we do not do it again. But it is foolish to dwell on past failures or past misfortunes. Not even God can change the past. We have to forgive ourselves and forgive others. Johann Goethe (1749-1831), Germany's greatest writer, said: "How could man live at all, if he did not give absolution every night to himself and all his brothers?" [1] No doubt God, if he exists, forgives us, as long as we are sorry for what we did and try to do better, so why be harsher than he? Marcus, the emperor, said:

> Don't feel despondent, if you don't always succeed in acting from right principles…rejoice, if overall your conduct is worthy of a man (or a woman).

We can compensate for wrongs we do to one person by doing good to another. We can compensate for disappointments, which have happened, by successes to fight for in the future. Some doctors have sleepless nights about their mistakes. What saves them is starting again with the next patient. Life always starts again today.

So when we sometimes fall short of our standards there is no need for us to be too hard on ourselves. Try again to be worthy of yourself and look to the future for happiness. When black thoughts come about past failure and wrongs done, as they do to all, put them quickly out of mind by concentrating on something else. If that does not work, tell yourself why it was not so important. Then think about your virtues and your successes. Finally think about other people's faults and failures.

We also have to forgive others, because nursing anger and resentment is not conducive to happiness. It adds extra harm to the injury done. Letting off steam in a diary can help. But forgive yourself more easily than you forgive others, because you know that you will try again but you do not know that they will. And forgive others with moderation, because forgiving too easily or too often makes us servile and lacking self-respect.

Anxiety within limits is sometimes necessary, because tension helps us to perform better and worry makes us take precautions. Unfortunately what hits us is usually the disaster we never considered. At times of stress anxiety is unavoidable. But excessive anxiety impairs performance as in stage fright. Anxiety, which cannot lead to useful action, only serves to make us unhappy. Once we are in the plane worry will not stop it crashing. Some people are troubled by free- floating anxiety, a feeling of tension about nothing in particular. Some have specific phobias for example about heights or about cancer.

Uncertainty creates anxiety, which is why we feel relieved when, for good or ill, the decision is taken and there is no going back. Religious fundamentalists are spared moral doubts. The uncertain and indecisive can find a guru to run their lives for them. But to be a proper human we must learn to live with some uncertainties.

This is a regime for combatting anxiety. You can do all components in sequence or any one of them in isolation.

1. Exercise
2. Diaphragmatic breathing
3. Muscle relaxation
4. Meditation

Exercise combats depression as well as anxiety. It can be just floor exercises at home, if it is part of the sequence.

Breathe with the diaphragm by lifting the abdomen as you inhale through the nose and collapse it as you breathe out through the mouth while counting the breaths as you do it.

Lie down comfortably and consciously relax all the muscles from head to toe in turn. The muscles round the eyes, the jaws, the fingers and toes are important. It may help to contract each muscle before relaxing it.

To meditate make your mind a blank or concentrate on some thought. Gently push away the extraneous thoughts, which will bombard you. It takes patience and persistence. Many books and discs give instructions on muscle relaxation and meditation.

You can try cognitive therapy on yourself. That means changing your way of thinking, more easily done with expert help. Tell yourself that few things matter very much and most do not really matter at all and what is troubling you may well come into the second category. Look at the worst and perhaps it is not so bad. If you cannot stop worrying about something, set aside half an hour to have a good worry about it and then get on with your life.

When all fails, ask your doctor for help. A family doctor may not have the time or the skill to offer you a course of cognitive therapy to help you to improve your way of thinking. A clinical psychologist can help both with general anxiety and specific phobias. The doctor may offer chemical help, which has its drawbacks. Do not try chemical help yourself by using that ancient remedy alcohol. The pleasant effects of alcohol do not last. The long term effects of repeated use do last.

Greed for pleasures or possessions is a danger to happiness; envy of the pleasures or possessions of others destroys it. To be envious is to resent being less happy in some way than someone else. However successful we are in any field, there will always be someone more successful. So concentrate your mind on those, who have done worse than you, not those, who have done better. The gap between your old car and his Mercedes is much smaller than the gap between you and the man without a car. Being a little poorer or a little richer has little effect on happiness but envy of someone richer certainly does. And few are successful in every field. His professional reputation outshines yours but your children are turning out better than his. Also you do not know his private problems and certainly not the future disasters, which may befall him.

Anger may be an appropriate emotion, even though it temporarily suppresses happiness. Jesus resorted to violence when he was disgusted by the moneychangers in the temple. [2] But excessive anger is negative. Road rage is an inappropriate response when another motorist cuts in on you in traffic. Accidents are avoided by your good driving not by improving his bad driving. Avoid useless anger. If you can't get even, try not to stay mad even though you get mad.

When we make mistakes we get angry with ourselves and our mistakes cause us more grief than our sins. We keep doing the same stupid or wrong things because we stay the same persons. Sometimes we find that we have just repeated the same mistake as before but with a new excuse. Or we have made a very similar mistake in a new situation. It is not easy to change our natures. We do have to accept what we are. Doctors make mistakes. The wrong kidney is taken from the right patient or the right kidney from the wrong patient. Then with righteous indignation a politician declares that this must never happen again. But the same mistake will happen again and again. Humans always make mistakes and the only way to reduce them is by improving systems. But humans can defeat the best system. We are as ingenious at finding wrong ways as right ways of doing things.

As for the future we need realistic optimism. Things may go reasonably well or improve somewhat. We also need discounted pessimism. The worst that may happen will not be so bad, unless we insist on making it so. And if you cannot change it, then try to lump it with as good a grace as possible. Never expect too much happiness. Denis Norden, the script writer, said that if he found his glasses in the morning, it was happiness enough for one day. Reduce the gap between expectation and reality. Think of your blessings, not your misfortunes. A happy family life and professional success do not always go together, and if either disappoint we must be grateful for the other. We must live in the here and now, in the present not the past or the future, even when the present task is mundane, like housework. Remember that, if you are unhappy with your lot for no good reason, a good reason may come.

And if you can't control the thoughts that make you unhappy, do the things that make you happy and then you won't have time for bad thoughts. [3]

MAKING OURSELVES HAPPY

It is hard to become a different person but we do have some control over the situations which we encounter, the actions, which we take, and even the thoughts on which we allow ourselves to dwell. For example many of us are awkward with social interactions and for that there are three remedies. We can try to improve by effort and practice. We can seek help and training. Or we can accept the problem and seek happiness in ways, which we find easier.

Gustave Flaubert, who wrote that great novel *Madame Bovary*, said that the recipe for a happy life was not too much intelligence, a little arrogance, and above all good health. But all aphorisms, including this one, are only partly true and only part of the truth. He was right about health, although some fine people stay happy without it. But good health certainly helps, if we want to take actions of any kind. I would have preferred it, if he had said confidence not arrogance. The latter hurts others and the former can be used to help them. He might have added a conscience, which is not too tender, because we are none of us perfect. He was right about intelligence. The clever people demand more of life and do not always get it. It is an analysis, not a recipe, because he does not offer guidance on the acquisition of the desirable traits.

Health

Being healthy is a pleasure because it feels good. It is also a duty because it gives you more energy to do things for others. We can improve our prospects in several ways. If you cannot do a lot for yourself, then do a little. What I tell you is right for most people and your doctor will tell you if it is right for you.

Your diet should concentrate on vegetables, fruit, fish, liquid vegetable oils, nuts, and whole grains. Omega-3 fatty acids, as in oily fish are good. Cut down on red meat, dairy products, and processed foods full of salt, fat and sugar. Avoid solid vegetable oils containing trans-fats. Cut down alcohol, if you drink more than me. A little regularly – about one glass of wine daily - probably does more good to your heart than harm to your liver. So why not enjoy it? Leave it one day a week to rest your liver and to show that you are in control, not the alcohol.

No smoking, except for a cigar at Christmas and birthdays. Try not to be too overweight. It makes women more unhappy than men, although it does more physical harm to men. But it is better to be fat and fit than thin and unfit.

Exercise is great. It lifts the spirits because it releases endorphin, a hormone with some morphine like properties. (I have had one injection of morphine and the sensation is beatific. That is what hooks addicts, who soon find that they need more and more just to avoid feeling dreadful.) Exercise is good for the health. It reduces the risk of heart trouble, diabetes and cancer. Moderate exercise enhances the immune system and reduces the number of colds we catch. It helps you keep weight down but only reducing calorie intake as well can make you lose weight. Surprisingly exercise delays dementia better than those brain training exercises in newspapers.

Start exercise slowly and take advice, if you are not used to it. Dynamic exercise is most important but doing a little static exertion against resistance also has a place.

- Frequency is more important than duration. Try to do it four to six times a week. Take at least one day off. From the best of things we need a rest. Half an hour to an hour is good. There is no call for most of us to do more and become athletes. But even a little is better than nothing. Climb a flight of stairs at work and take short walks when opportunity presents.
- Don't go at it too fiercely. You should be breathing more deeply than usual but able to hold a conversation during exercise. Your pulse rate should be roughly 90-120 beats a minute [(220 minus age) times 0.6 to 0.8].
- Cycling, swimming, jogging and walking are good, because you are in control of your effort. Don't drop dead competing on the squash court. Walking is best because you just step out of your front door in your street clothes.
- With both exercise and diet start a regime that you will be able to continue.

You may wonder why exercise and the diet suggested should be healthy. It is probably because our ancestors were physically active, faced calorie lack, not calorie abundance, and had no access to the salt and refined sugar we love. That is the lifestyle for which our bodies were designed. So we should introduce into our sedentary lifestyles ordinary activity, like gardening, housework and DIY jobs as well as more specific exercise.

If you don't like Western style aerobic exercise, singing in a choir is good for the health as are the Eastern practices like yoga and Tai Chi. You are more likely to have success if you start by joining a class. Mindfulness is a new approach. We concentrate on what we are doing in the present moment and enjoy its interest, its beauty, or its peace. It seems rather obvious. Whatever you decide on you have to like it to stick with it year after year.

> My father's hobby was visiting houses for sale posing as a prospective purchaser, which by a very elastic definition he was. He said that he rarely saw a loft without a disused exercise bicycle in it.

See your doctor. The advice she gives you now may be outdated in ten years' time. It will not be as outdated as the advice she would have given you ten years' ago; medicine advances. Most of us seem to need statins for our cholesterol levels and blood pressure pills as we grow older. Physical inactivity, obesity, smoking, poor diet and chronic stress shorten life. Your doctor cannot cure those for you.

Your mental state affects your health by changing the production of the stress hormones, cortisol and adrenaline. They are needed for acute stresses but a prolonged excess is damaging. Be optimistic and trusting rather than suspicious but be careful of the telephone and internet rogues out there. Think well of yourself and feel that your life has meaning.

Pleasures

Everyone should allow himself pleasure, when he can, because frequent experience of pleasure helps to make us happy. Pleasure is temporary and ecstasy is brief but they do contribute to happiness.

We must not excuse ourselves from the duties, which we expect of others, but we should also allow ourselves the pleasures, which we would permit to others. So delight in them with a clear conscience. It is stupid and wrong to deny yourself legitimate pleasures; they make for happiness and happiness is a duty.

> Man will hereafter be called to account for depriving himself of the good things, which the world lawfully allows. [4]

Perhaps the rabbi, who said this, was thinking of the girls he ungallantly failed to kiss before he married and the ones he treacherously kissed afterwards or perhaps not.

Most of us want to enjoy a good meal, a glass or two of wine, a good book, and especially sex, that most intense physical pleasure of all. Why deprive yourself of pleasure, if it harms no one and is consistent with duty? It should trouble us that many better than us lead far more miserable lives. There is no point in letting it trouble us so much that it spoils our legitimate pleasures. Just do a little to help.

Pleasure may be idiosyncratic. It may come from owning the largest matchbox collection in the world, if that is what turns you on. The joy of any collection is continuing it, not completing it. If gold is your goal you may be happy sitting on a swelling heap of it. But once you stop accumulating the only sensible thing to do is to give it away.

Certainly physical pleasure alone can never bring happiness. They say that the life devoted to it is the most strenuous of all. Gluttony brings indigestion and satyriasis causes impotence. Aristotle (484-322 BC) said:

> Happiness is not found in amusement; for it would be absurd, if the end were amusement, and our lifelong efforts and sufferings aimed at amusing ourselves. [5]

The physical pleasures are brief though some might think them sufficient for happiness but it is an impoverished happiness. Spiritual pleasures, such as music, literature and art last longer.

> Aldous Huxley in his book *Ape and Essence* describes an elderly millionaire's search for longevity. Obispo, an unscrupulous scientist, is helping him and is also researching the private regions of the millionaire's nubile friend. Obispo thinks that eating powdered carp guts might be the answer, because of the longevity of carp. He finds that a noble earl was on the same track two hundred years before. They gain access to a secret room in the family castle, guarded by the earl's descendants. There they find the earl and his spouse turned into apes and enjoying sexual congress. The millionaire recovers from his shock and remarks that they are having a good time. Obispo just laughs. [6]

The two morals are that we should not seek longevity at all cost and we should not sacrifice the spiritual to the physical. We do not live by bread alone or by bread and circuses or by bread, circuses and sex. Many of us need something more. The philosopher, G E Moore (1873-1958) thought that the supreme goods for a human were social intercourse and the contemplation of beauty. Beauty can be seen in ballroom dancing or in modern art, in jazz or classical music, in poetry or in nature. All can transport us into another world for a time. I would widen Moore's claim to getting engrossed in any activity or doing something useful for others. Nobody finds happiness by seeking it. We must seek what brings it and enjoyable occupations are important and what you enjoy is usually what you are good at.

> If you observe a really happy man you will find him building a boat, writing a symphony, educating his son, growing double dahlias in his garden. [7]

Relationships

They are more important than wealth and professional success. Lasting happiness comes from a happy marriage to one, who started as your lover and has become also your best friend and your partner in life's enterprise. A loving, cheerful spouse is a boon, which all should seek. But if he or she does not measure up, remember that neither do you. Happiness is about making the most of the fairly good, not yearning for the perfect.

It also takes compromise. What do you do, if your spouse hates the city and you hate the country? What do you do, if your job is engrossing and demanding but your spouse wants you to devote more time to him or her and the children? You have to find the compromise, which offers benefit to both.

There is profound satisfaction from seeing our children happy. But happiness for you may not be happiness for them. You yearn to return to your village in Ireland but you have raised your children in London? They may accept the village as a holiday place but they will be aghast at the prospect of life there. You have to accept that they go their own way and maintain family closeness by frequent visits.

It is good to have close friends, with whom you can discuss problems. It is good to have a busy social life involving a wider circle. By networking we learn useful things and hear many opinions. Social intercourse can be part of drinking in the pub or thoughtful discussion in a book club. A strong social network, as religious congregations provide, can compensate for many difficulties. Church attenders are happier than others. They have social contact and mutual support. I read that the prostitutes in the brothels of Calcutta were surprisingly happy, despite their miserable, exploited lives, because of their support of and affection for each other. Cooperating with others in any task makes us happy, which is perhaps why depression disappears in wartime. It is sad that it can take a war to bring purpose and happiness to some. There is prolonged satisfaction in feeling useful to others. So avoid social isolation. Summon up the energy and get involved. There is much information about groups in the local libraries. But what is important is not the extent of your social circle but your personal satisfaction with it.

Altruistic behaviour

Acts of kindness without hope of material reward bring emotional reward and what matters is the way you feel inside you, not the possessions you have around you.

- Altruistic behaviour increases life satisfaction.
- Most of us have experienced that little feeling of pleasure, which comes when we do someone an

easy, minor good turn, like giving someone the right directions.

- We need to feel that our lives have some purpose and meaning. Helping others can give them that meaning.
- There are health benefits in volunteering to do good works.
- Most of us are unhappy when we act wrongly, because few people have no conscience. We are happier when we succeed in doing the right thing.

Acts of kindness make us happier and they make those we help happier. Their happiness returns to us and spreads to yet others. Goodness and happiness are closely connected. Our personal happiness is an integral part of the happiness of humanity. We look at the world through our own eyes but, as rational creatures, we should also stand outside the world and see ourselves as part of it. We are somewhere between the animals and the angels. We care for others but put our own interests before theirs unless we love them.

Money

There is no misery which is not made worse by poverty. That being said, having more than enough makes you no happier than having enough. When you are poor a little makes you a lot happier but when you are not, it takes a lot to make you a little happier. It is true of the individual and true of the nation. One study showed that people did not grow happier when their yearly income rose above 50,000 dollars. That figure must seem like paradise to those subsisting on two dollars a day. On a national level studies show that we have grown much richer in the UK since 1975 but no happier. People are overall happier and healthier in egalitarian countries, like the Scandinavian ones, than in countries like the US, where the difference between the rich and the poor is much wider. I put the suicides in Sweden down to the long winters.

Those who value people more than possessions, tend to be happier. Some have become accustomed to the trappings of conspicuous consumption, large cars, large houses, long haul holidays and meals in smart restaurants, to name a few luxuries. Actually we enjoy luxuries more, if we enjoy them less often. If champagne is an occasional treat, it is a better treat than when we drink it every day. Luxury should be enjoyed with amused contempt, never mourning its loss in a recession, because others lack even the necessities.

Work

Doing the job that you know you should be doing, the one that is right for your personality and your talent, is very important as most of us spend much of our lives at work. It is good to be a little, round peg in a little, round hole. Thomas Aquinas (1224-74), the greatest theologian of the Catholic Church, said that we each had a particular purpose directly related to each person's talents and abilities, "that one talent, which is death to hide". [8] Having some choice about how we go about our work reduces stress. Being happy at work makes it easier to look outwards and think of others, which in turn makes us happier.

Talent for the work is not enough. There is no success without opportunity, instruction, and example, for which you are dependent on others. Mozart would not have been Mozart, if his father had been a farm labourer. Hard work is even more essential, and within our own control. Newton said that he made his discoveries by thinking constantly about the problems.

We do not all have the good fortune to do the work we should be doing. Those condemned to boring, repetitive work in industrial society are alienated from it, as Karl Marx (1818-83) describing Victorian industry, emphasised. But happiness can still come from camaraderie at work, from the honour of supporting a family, and from our lives outside work. Don't expect to win on all counts.

Reaching for a star

Some people are prepared to sacrifice their lives and even the lives of those near to them to follow their star. The painter Paul Gauguin followed his star to Tahiti, leaving his family behind. Gauguin produced great art but what if posterity had found him mediocre. The failures do not become great names so we do not know about them. But were they more wrong to try than those who succeeded? The French have a saying that remorse is better than regret, and it applies not only to love.

Difficulty comes when reaching for one's own star clashes with other duties, usually the duty to care for the welfare of those closest to us. We always have to make choices. Nelson Mandela was imprisoned for 27 years. He suffered greatly because he was unable to look after his wife and children. When he came out of prison his daughter was the same age as her mother was when he went to prison. Our admiration is enhanced because his sacrifice freed his nation. What if he had died in gaol with his mission unaccomplished? Aung San Su Kyi could not be with her husband during his final illness nor with her children as they grew up. She could not leave Burma because the Junta would probably have not let her return. Lately there is a little hope that her sacrifice will also be rewarded.

All those who reach for some star, must decide how much to sacrifice in the quest. The choice between duty and personal satisfaction is difficult. We need to know the importance of the goal to ourselves. We need to ask ourselves whether success would bring a purely personal satisfaction or whether it would benefit others. We must consider whether there is a reasonable chance of achieving the goal. Is it a genuine prospect or a mirage? We should not put our dream before all responsibility. We should follow our star but not regardless of all else, not regardless of all duties.

No political cause is without dangers. The revolution eats its children and everyone else's; freed American slaves were sent to Liberia where they enslaved others. The single act of kindness is least likely to disappoint, provided no gratitude is expected. We, who are not driven and pursue modest goals, should remember that.

3

Why Happiness Is The Ultimate Good

Is happiness the supreme good? Should we seek our own happiness above all else and promote other people's as the chief benefit we can confer on them? That is what the eccentric English, philosopher Jeremy Bentham (1748-1832) thought. He considered any other approach to morality "nonsense on stilts." But Immanuel Kant, the equally eccentric German philosopher, thought obedience to the moral law was the supreme good, irrespective of its effect on our own or anyone else's happiness. He spoke of his wonder at "the starry heaven above me and the moral law within me." [1]

I side largely with Bentham. Acting rightly and obeying the moral law must have a final purpose. What can that purpose be, if it is not the general happiness of all? If it is just to get to heaven, it does seem rather selfish. If you think that God commanded us to obey certain moral laws, he must have had some object in mind. What was that object, if it was not the general happiness? There has to be an end user, someone who benefits from our obedience to moral laws and the benefit that person is most likely to want is an increase in his happiness. What is the point of living if you are not happy, nor are you making others happy?

Look at it the other way. If we all obeyed a moral code and it made everybody thoroughly miserable, would there not be something wrong with that code? So we are judging our morality by its effect on happiness. Some might argue that we would necessarily be happy, if we followed the right moral code whatever that might be. But we can all recognise happiness and we certainly do not agree about which is the right moral code. Puritans think they follow the right moral code but they are not renowned for their happiness. If following our moral principles does not bring happiness, either we are following our principles too slavishly or happiness is not important. We must consider carefully which is more likely. I discount claims about lives beyond this one, for which there is no evidence.

When he died Bentham had himself dissected at a public anatomy lecture. He clearly thought that death did not end our duty to the public good. His skeleton was then padded with hay and displayed in a wooden cabinet in University College, London. His head was originally at his feet but it is now locked away because the students vandalised it. Even death does not protect philosophers. The head currently on his shoulders is made of wax. He still attends college meetings on major anniversaries, when he is recorded as present but not voting. He is the one, who never says anything stupid.

Challenges to the primacy of happiness

Is it enough to promote mindless, irresponsible happiness with no care for others? In H G Wells' novel *The Time Machine*, set in the future, the Eloi, who had evolved from the humans of today, were like that. But in the end encouraging irresponsibility would be self-defeating, because none of us would finish happy, if none of us cared about the happiness of others. The duty to promote happiness has to be farsighted. We have a duty to try to be happy. We have a duty to make others happy. We have a duty to make them happy in a way, which will encourage them to make yet others happy, which includes us.

Does not learning have intrinsic importance? But what use is learning unless it benefits someone, even if it is only the learner? It is hard to see who would be happier, if I understood quantum mechanics and the rest of modern physics, unless it made me happier. It would make no one else happier for sure and as it would make me no happier I will not bother even to try.

Is not beauty intrinsically valuable? There may be symmetry and colour but there is no beauty, unless someone appreciates it. The beauty is in the mind of the observer. When a tree falls in an empty forest there are sound waves. There is no sound, because there is no hearer. A hidden Vermeer is no use to anyone until it is discovered. It would be pointless to play a recording of a Mozart symphony to an empty desert. All the spiritual and intellectual pleasures, indeed all pleasures, are important because people enjoy them.

Is friendship a good in itself? We derive physical and emotional benefit from our friendships. We give and we get. We take pleasure in doing good to each other. We have an especial duty to benefit our friends, because of our moral closeness to them. A destructive friendship, which damages one or both parties, gives no happiness and does no good. It is a relationship rather than a friendship. Friendship is important only as a source of happiness.

Are not the virtues of courage, steadfastness, determination, wisdom, prudence, patience and loyalty goods to be desired? Actually they are qualities, which wicked people can use to destroy the happiness of others. Was loyalty to Hitler a good? Goering said that Adolf Hitler was his conscience. Contrary to what people like to think I have known bullies who were quite brave. However, once the duty to promote happiness has been accepted, they are important adjuncts to it and so become instrumentally good. Qualities and virtues are good, only when they are used for right ends.

Is not justice important whether anyone benefits or not? There is a famous maxim "let justice be done though the heavens fall". It seems to say that justice should take priority over happiness. Can that challenge be met? Consider distributive justice, sharing out benefits. That aspect of justice is just a subsidiary principle controlling the way that goods, which promote happiness, are conferred.

Punitive justice presents a more difficult challenge. Should not a criminal be punished, even if punishing him benefits no one? We think that punishment should reform the criminal and we would like to think that he would be happier, if he reformed. Crime harms people and punishment deters it and so preserves their happiness. But we still think that crime should be punished simply because crime deserves punishment. Our society would deteriorate, if we felt no need to reward the good and punish the bad. So justice is still an instrumental good. Nevertheless, irrespective of all that, we still think that it is intrinsically right to punish wickedness. Kant was partly right about the intrinsic importance of morality.

Whose view of happiness?

In general we should accept that each of us knows best what makes him or her happy. We are each of us experts on ourselves and the professional experts know only what suits most people. You want to listen to Bach and I want to rock around the clock. We should respect each other's wishes and not impose what we consider to be benefits on other people.

> An energetic assistant started work for a consultant surgeon. After six months he proudly announced to his boss that he had cleared his waiting list completely. The man exploded with rage. "If I have no waiting list, people will think that I am no good."

I am, however, entitled to decide that what you want would harm you or harm others and decline to do it. I will not supply you with crack cocaine.

Bentham regarded all pleasures as equally valuable, and famously said that pushpin, a simple board game, was as good as poetry. John Stuart Mill (1806-73), a leading follower of Bentham, thought that higher pleasures, the intellectual ones, were deeper and of longer duration than pure physical pleasures. He thought that they were intrinsically more valuable. After all he was a philosopher and studied ancient Greek at the age of three. They do tend to be of longer duration but it is difficult to see why the happiness, which comes from physical experience should be necessarily inferior to happiness coming from more lofty pursuits.

We can, however, say that a human who has acquired a little culture and learning, is unlikely to be satisfied with just animal pleasures. It is also the duty of those who educate him, to encourage him to acquire the learning so that he will be able to enjoy spiritual as well as basic pleasures. When he can enjoy higher pleasures, he will probably not be satisfied with just the basic physical ones. Nevertheless it might be hard to show that the man, who enjoys ogling pin-ups is less happy than the one, who listens to Bach, or indeed that he spreads less happiness around him.

> It is better to be a human being dissatisfied than a pig satisfied; better to be Socrates dissatisfied than a fool satisfied. And if the fool or the pig are of a different opinion, it is because they only know their own side of the question. The other party knows both sides. [2]

That is what Mill thought. So he thought that it was better to be unhappy, if happiness consisted purely in enjoying basic, animal pleasures. But if the fool is satisfied, harms no one and fulfils his duties what is the harm? "Where ignorance is bliss it is folly to be wise." Is it really better to be an unhappy intellectual than a happy simpleton?

In general each is entitled to his own view of happiness provided that it harms no one. That does not apply to children in our care. Adults usually know better than children and they are responsible for the future of the children. I have carried a grandchild howling to the car to take him to school only to see him jump out of the car minutes later to join his friends in the playground.

We also have no right to try to impose the happiness of salvation in the hereafter on anyone. There are three objections to doing so. There is no proof that anyone enjoys posthumous bliss. There is no agreement as to which belief will secure bliss. We have no right to impose our will on others.

Is action necessary to create happiness?

I can make myself happy with my thoughts alone but I cannot make you happy without communicating those thoughts in words. Words are actions; they comfort, advise, cheer us, and encourage us to benefit others. And a cruel word may be more painful than a blow. Words have effects as the inquisition knew and all other dictatorships know. They could not stop Galileo thinking that the earth went round the sun and they probably did not care what he thought. But they certainly stopped him saying it.

Someone can be benefited by indirect action. I benefit Tom, if I encourage Fred to help him. I also put myself in a position to help others more, if I increase my knowledge or improve my health.

Pious Christian and Buddhist monks spend their days in contemplation and prayer; do they increase happiness in the world? They live harmless, satisfied lives and that is good in itself. They support their fellow monks. They show the rest of us obsessed with material goods, which we do not need, that there is another way. So what they are doing does promote happiness without obvious action, although they do still better when they help the sick and the poor.

You are distraught, because your son is dangerously ill. You spend an hour in church praying for him. You come out feeling more peaceful.

Is prayer a good action, which promotes happiness, even if there is no response to it? You have benefited, and that is in itself good. We are allowed to take a God's eye view of the world and see ourselves as one of the multitude needing help. There is no duty to ask less for oneself than for others. Our own peace of mind is an intrinsic good. Prayer can also be an action instrumental to helping others. A feeling of peace helps us deal with all situations and people better. If your mental or physical health benefits, you can do more.

We can do good by deliberate inaction, sometimes as important as action. Thomas Aquinas, said: "He could have acted, and he did not." In other words we are responsible for what we do not do, as much as for what we actually do. Intentional inaction is just as much a moral choice and can have just as powerful effect on happiness as action. Refusing to spread the slander reduces unhappiness. Refusing to evade tax helps the community. But there can be a moral difference between causing a similar effect by action or by inaction.

> A contemporary philosopher, asked what the difference was between sending five plates of poisoned food to five starving people, and not sending enough money to save five people from starvation. Five die just the same. [3]

Deliberately killing and deliberately letting die have the same effect but are not quite the same morally. When we send poisoned food we actually want people to die. But when we do not send money for famine relief, we do not want anyone to die. We alone are responsible for the poison, but there are others, who have a greater responsibility than us to relieve the famine. But if they refuse to do it, then perhaps we must.

> I used to take my neighbour's garbage sack to the communal bin every week because he was even more decrepit than me. I saw his garbage sack outside his door as usual but his daughter's bicycle was also there. So I went to the shops and on my return the bicycle was gone but the sack was not. I could only laugh and shoulder the sack.

I deserve more blame for the unhappiness I cause than for the unhappiness I do not relieve. I must not steal the lifebelt from you to save myself. I do not have to surrender mine to you and let myself drown. We are not obliged to devote ourselves exclusively to good works, but we should always try to avoid harming anyone.

These distinctions between action and inaction do not apply, when there is special responsibility. The doctor looking after the patient cannot neglect him, and then claim that it was the disease that killed him, because she has a special responsibility to act and intervene. The pregnant woman cannot say that her baby is welcome to go to another womb. Refusing to throw you a lifebelt when I see you drowning is almost as bad as pushing you overboard.

Happiness, intention and motive

Intention is the desired effect of an action. I gave you the poisoned apple so that you would eat it and die. Motive is why it is done. I hated you.

There is reason to be happy, if we do someone good because our intention and our motive were to do so. Why not also be happy, if we make someone happy, even when it was not our intention? We can take pleasure in what we have done for others, even when our motives were not quite pure, even when they were largely selfish. Life comes at us in shades of grey, not usually black and white. The lifesaver works for money but is happy to save life. Do you care why he has saved you? And if he gets into the habit of saving life on duty he will do it on his day off. We are creatures of habit.

There are two tests we can apply, if we want to examine our motives, although it is difficult to see why we should. I will apply them to a trivial, chauvinistic example.

> Your wife needs a holiday and you would rather like one too, but not enough to justify the expense, if she had not wanted it.

Would you have booked the holiday just for your own sake, if she had not wanted it? If so, it was not a good action. Would you have booked it just for her, if you had not wanted it also? If so, it was a good action. If pleasing her tipped the balance, you can congratulate yourself on modest goodness. "We are not wholly bad or wholly good, who live our lives under Milk Wood." [4] But whichever motive predominated why not be happy that she is happy?

Often it happens the other way round. We mean well and we cause trouble. We should try not to make ourselves unhappy when that happens. The world runs on probabilities. It is not a failure of goodness, when benevolent action, taken after careful consideration, turns out to cause unhappiness. Kant said that only intentions count:

> A good will is not good because of what it effects or accomplishes… it is good through its willing alone. [5]

In other words we should not make ourselves unhappy when our good intentions have bad results. If we help the little old lady across the road, and she gets mugged on the other side, we have still done a good deed. We can neither foresee nor control all the effects of our actions. We can harm with good motives, even when it is entirely reasonable to think that we are promoting happiness. We must let probability rule us.

> In recent years pretty girls have offered me their seats on the bus. They have no idea of the chagrin they cause by emphasising my age. My feet are rested but my pride is dented. To fill my bitter cup a man with greying hair gave his seat to me on the bus in France this year. Gratitude came through gritted teeth. My wife feels the same now that our ten-year-old grandson has taken to helping her up the stairs. She is charmed but not quite ready for it.

However, the old proverb says that the road to hell is paved with good intentions. It is simply not enough to mean well. We must also consider very carefully the possible results of our actions.

Friedrich Hegel (1770-1831) introduced a useful concept. He claimed that knowledge advanced by a process of thesis, antithesis, and then synthesis.

Hegel was a German philosopher of impenetrable obscurity and why he was so much admired in the nineteenth century it is hard to understand. He progressed from a revolutionary youth to a reactionary old age but that I can understand more easily.

Kant advanced the thesis that only intention counts; the old proverb provides the antithesis that good intentions may lead to disaster. The synthesis is that wisdom must control intention. It is a reconciliation of the opposing assertions, and provides a new thesis for someone else to oppose.

If we make no one unhappy, can we still be doing something wrong? Can an action be wrong, if it has no harmful effect on anyone?

> You promise your best friend on his deathbed that you will climb his favourite mountain to scatter his ashes from it. Puffing away you toil upwards, wondering whether to throw the ashes into the nearest stream. Neither he nor anyone else would know.

If we break faith on this occasion, we are more likely to do it again, when it will cause harm. We risk reducing our capacity to promote happiness.

> A man and woman meet, fall in love, and resolve to marry. Then they find that they are brother and sister, separated at birth. They marry nevertheless, without revealing their kinship and agreeing not to have children.

They defend their decision. Their partnership will bring them happiness and strengthen their abilities to do good in the world. There is no need for children in an overpopulated world. The need for secrecy is a problem for society, not them. Breaking this law will not encourage them or others to break other laws.

Brother and sister matings are biologically and socially unwise. Incest is likely to disturb the harmony of a nuclear family as well as producing abnormal children. Natural selection has made us averse to coupling with those, with whom we are raised. This is also true of unrelated children raised collectively but not true of this incestuous couple. The law cannot be changed for every hard case. But are they morally right that their happiness alone counts or is there a moral law not to be broken? My answer is that they are taking a dangerous step, which they should not do. I am not of the romantic school, which believes that there is only one perfect partner for each of us.

4

Growing Old And Staying Happy

General de Gaulle said that old age was a shipwreck but we may beach on a pleasant shore. Many of us are already quite old but sometimes we can forget it and feel quite young again. If you can forget that you are old, even for a short time, be grateful.

We must accept old age with amused tolerance. It comes just as fast if you don't. With age we learn to be happy with less, with less health, less income, and less fun. It is easier to accept having less, as we grow older. Less can also be better, less responsibility and less concern about what others think. First we stop caring what they think about us and then we realise that actually they never were thinking about us.

Age has many compensations. Grandchildren are one; lessening of the competitive drive is another. We become cynical about Kipling's "twin impostors, triumph and disaster". We accept what we are and the limitations of our achievement. The failures, which pained us in middle age, no longer seem important. We have more leisure to do what we enjoy. We have a good excuse not to rush from one job to the next. Time fills nicely by doing things more slowly and resting between activities. We also have time, patience, and realism. We still have a duty to fulfil the responsibilities appropriate to our age but age also relieves us from some responsibilities of middle age. And we must continue to enjoy the pleasures, which age has not taken away.

Physical changes

Age creeps up on us unawares, until some event forces it on our attention. There is a gradual decline in all functions, physical, mental, social, and sexual, which may happen without us realising it. Suddenly we find we cannot climb the slope, which we hardly noticed ten years before. Or like me you fall off the stepping stones, which you tried to cross one last time, despite the warnings of your spouse. Sleep comes easily by day and only fitfully at night. Acute problems like muscle strains and minor viral infections take so much longer to recover. And more and more chronic physical problems latch onto us obliging us to swallow an increasing number of tablets each day. Everything nasty happens with increasing frequency as we age.

Physical attractiveness declines, which is less of a problem to those, who have always had to rely on a capacity to appeal by being amusing, not by looking good. We face the mirror on the wall and in it you see your jowls and either your stringy neck or your double chin. Choose whichever you prefer. The ageing face looks better with a little extra fat. A woman wrote in a magazine that when she reached forty, she knew that she had to choose between her face and her bottom. As men no longer looked at her bottom, she chose her face. Cosmetic surgery is not the answer to age but I see no sin in the rare, selective repair, such as having the bags under your eyes improved. But frequent plastic surgery just makes people look odd and evidences an immature approach to the stages of life.

The ageing process has a macabre interest for doctors, as they can watch it in their own skins. The main cause of skin ageing is age, which is the main cause of all ageing. You can do nothing about it. Three things, however, Increase the rate at which our skins age. They are North European ancestry, about which you can also do nothing, and sun and smoking, about which you can do something. But be moderate, because the suns helps us to make vitamin D and lifts our spirits, and the occasional cigar is not so sinful.

Vertical and horizontal furrows appear on the forehead and around the nose and mouth. The barber offers to trim your eyebrows, because hair seems to grow well everywhere, except where you want it. Blobs grow on our skins; little polyps and little red spots, called senile haemangiomas. Large, brown blotches spread on the face and the backs of the hands. The doctors call them senile freckles, which is what they are; the Americans call them liver spots, which is what they look like; the English call them grave marks and the French call them cemetery medals, which is what they foretell. Little bruises spread and go purple; that is called senile purpura. Worst of all, the skin itches for no obvious reason; they call it senile pruritus. This insistence on senility is clinical rather than kind.

The changing room of the local sports centre offers opportunities to observe the ravages of age in others, which is a more congenial pastime than observing our own. And there are a lot of old men in changing rooms trying to slow the inevitable physical decline by exercise. We old gentlemen are all the same. We diminish; we lose height; legs are skinny; buttocks shrink; posture is bent; only bellies enlarge. Chivalry dissuades me from describing old ladies, and if I were allowed into the female changing room, younger ladies might disturb my observations. Marilyn Monroe and Princess Diana are icons of feminine beauty, because no one has ever seen them old, but the price of not withering is being plucked. Senile decay and disintegration will come but let us have fun until they do.

Thus, though we cannot make our sun

Stand still, yet we will make him run. [1]

Retirement

Acquaintances, who see you infrequently, say that you look ten years younger when they see you after you retire. It is true but it is just a blip in the ageing process, because you will continue ageing from the new point, although hopefully at a slower rate.

The reward for sticking with a difficult job is the sheer bliss of retiring from it. The price for loving your work may be fear of leaving it. You lose your status and your purpose in life, and you have not acquired other interests, because the job was so engrossing. Some businessmen have a particular problem, if they lack the intellectual interests, which are so useful after working life ends. It is worse, when they have grown rich, and have become used to paying others to do their decorating and household repairs, which the rest of us quite liked doing, even when we worked. They become more important in retirement. Faced with this problem, small businessmen continue working until they lose their money, and big businessmen go on until they lose other people's money.

We should work at the level of our ability so we should seize the opportunity to change to less onerous work in the years before retirement, if we get the chance. So often we do not. Experience and wisdom may increase but physical and mental agility and receptiveness to new ideas decline. So try to achieve a demotion, preferably one disguised as a promotion, before retirement. It is easier to jump off the tree from a lower branch.

The duty to retire gradually increases, as you realise that you are not quite as good at the job as you were and slowly getting worse. Sadly we do not all have the insight to realise it. Boxing champions often go on until they are knocked out. The most successful politicians are usually forced out of office by some final failure. Both roles need self-belief, including the delusion that no one can replace you. There was an Australian news editor, who never took a holiday for two reasons. First he thought that they would never manage without him and second he thought that they would. I was better than the young doctors at making reflective decisions, but was falling increasingly behind them at the emergency work. It was time to go. There is always someone younger pleased to occupy your place and probably able to do the job better. Still old doctors make up in understanding what they lack in modernity.

When I started work, I did not believe in retirement and thought that life meant working until you were sixty-five and then dying. As years went by that prospect grew increasingly unpalatable. We scorn the idea of pensions, when we are young, and spend our middle years regretting having done so. Once you think about retiring then do so as soon as you can afford it. The catch with postponing your pension to enlarge it is that you may not live to spend it. The problem with the financial calculation is that you do not know how long you will live. Our guesses are inevitably wrong, and money runs out before life or life runs out before money. The old may be mean with themselves, because they find it hard to see their savings reduce, even though they know that accumulating money in old age is pointless. The young need to control the tendency to overspend and the old to underspend.

Poverty may build the character in youth but there is nothing to be said for it in old age. It is a disaster to need money from family when you are old. "When the father gives to the son both laugh and when the son gives to the father both cry." But the adage is partly false. You want to give to your son to help him with the deposit on the house but not because he has lost his job. If your son has struck it rich, you are happy to boast about the luxuries he has provided for you, but would rather not need him for the necessities.

If you are a man, who has worked long hours, and your wife has concentrated on the home, both you and your spouse must adjust to the new situation. Life has changed for you but not for her; she has not retired. If you move into a smaller house, consistent with your altered situation, she will find your ubiquity even more painful. If you interfere in the running of the house, she will suggest that you go back to work. She wants a humble assistant to relieve her of menial tasks, not a supervisor.

Do not haunt the old workplace; they are still busy and have no time to chat. If I saw one retired surgeon approaching along the corridor, I had to pretend I had not seen him and nip up a flight of stairs to the corridor above. Many used this ploy. Neither must you haunt the house of a married child. The parents of young children are busy, especially when both work. So go when invited or when they call you to help.

Staying happy

What you need to enjoy yourself is health, a little wealth, some friends and best of all a loving companion. Enjoy them while you can, because one of them will vanish soon enough. Each day try to do something useful to others, something pleasant, something physical, something intellectual and something social. It is not as hard as it sounds because missing a day does not matter and one activity, such as a serious discussion, can fulfil two functions. Get out of the house every day. Keep busy; it is good in general and leaves less time to snack. Voluntary work is a way of helping both yourself and others.

Maintain your independence. Stay in your own home as long as you can, even though you are frail, and let the children worry about you falling. You may fall anyway in the nursing home. Only people who have lived very hard lives, want to end them cared for in an institution, however comfortable it might be. But move to a more suitable home while you are still young enough to do it. Unfortunately we either move before we really need to or leave it until we just can't face it. Stairs are good exercise until you get too old to climb them. Walk-in showers, special chairs and high toilet seats help. Most important is a supportive network.

Use your free bus pass instead of the car. When you leave it in the garage you can bask in a glow of ecological virtue. It is pleasant to flash your pass and ride for free; it is relaxing to let someone else do the driving and look out of the window. There is a better view from the top deck than there is from a car and you have the leisure to enjoy it. It is a little embarrassing to see young women, possibly poorer than you, dip into their purses for the fare while dragging their children behind them. That is not your doing.

Attitude is important. G K Chesterton advised us not to "prolong the folly of youth to be the shame of age". Dylan Thomas told us not to "go gently into that goodnight." You can usually find a quotation to support whatever point you want to make about ageing and indeed about most things. It takes wisdom to know when to follow which advice. The Welshman is more often right. Take the adventure holiday and let the children stay at home and worry about you. You worried enough about their adventures. They mainly worry about their feelings of guilt but you will worry about their welfare, even as they drive you to the nursing home.

Duties remain. You must not just enjoy yourself, and you will probably not do so, if enjoyment is your only aim. There may be grandchildren to care for. I worked part time at the blood donation centre for a few years, mainly because there was a staff shortage, although the pay was quite welcome. It happened because a former colleague recognised me as I lay peacefully bleeding and her boss gave me an interview and a job, before I rose from the couch. No doubt many would give two pints of blood these days to get a job so easily. I was never good with my hands, sometimes a source of worry at work, and it is strange how what you fear chases after you. On the one hand we should do good in the way that suits us best but on the other we should do the good that comes our way.

Staying healthy

The health rules are much the same as they were but you find yourself visiting the doctor once every few months, not once in a blue moon. Continue with physical activity, albeit with gradually reducing intensity but not reducing frequency. If you have never been physically active, then start now but gradually and with advice. Non-competitive exercise is boring but safer than competitive games as activity is under your own control. As the joints wear out swimming may be all that is left. Relax about unhealthy food. You will not live forever, however hard you try. Old men should sit down when they get up in the night to pass water. If you stand and look up at the ceiling, you may faint.

There is an old medical joke that the only healthy man is one, who has not yet been fully investigated. People are becoming increasingly enthusiastic about screening tests, looking for problems they never knew they had. They hope to be reassured that they are healthy or failing that discover some hidden disease, which can be nipped in the bud by modern treatment. Sadly not all screening tests are a good idea for all people.

- It is only worth screening for diseases which are reasonably common.
- There has to be some benefit in finding the disease before it causes symptoms. So it must be treatable and

better treated early than late or people are subjected to worry without benefit.

- The test has to be fairly sensitive to the presence of the disease. Otherwise there is false and dangerous reassurance.
- It has to be fairly specific for the disease or many without the disease are subjected to unpleasant, unnecessary tests, and needless anxiety.

The ideal screening test is checking your blood pressure. If it is normal, you can be reassured. If it is high, treatment will benefit you. It is also worth having your urine checked with a dipstick for sugar, protein and blood and the stool for blood. There are advantages and disadvantages with some other screening tests. Some think that older men should have an abdominal ultrasound to detect asymptomatic aneurysms. If such an aneurysm bursts, the outlook is grave. But not every aneurysm will burst and operation before it bursts also has its risks. Opinion differs as to whether men should have a blood test for prostate cancer in the absence of a family history. Early treatment saves life. But not all prostate cancers are invasive. You must decide with your doctor whether any particular screening test is a good idea for you.

Sleep

When older patients complained to me about their sleep when I was a young doctor I asked them whether they could run as fast as they did. Of course it is true that sleep, like so much else, must deteriorate with age but my response was neither kind nor useful. There is something to be said for old doctors, who know a little more about what happens to us in life.

Sleep rules are simple. Do not sleep anywhere except in bed at night. Use your bed only for sleep, not for any other relaxation except sex. If you are getting both sleep and sex, be very grateful. Go to bed and get up at set times, even at weekends. Make occasional exceptions to almost every rule. Look at the websites about insomnia.

Living longer

There are usually choices in life, like being hanged or being shot. None of the choices may appeal. Either grow old or do not grow old. Suffer the sadness of seeing your friends die or let the sadness be theirs. Try to be altruistic and bear the sadness yourself. But if you live too long you outlive your spouse, your friends, and worst of all, even your children. Do you want to live to see them as old people, waiting for you to be off, especially, if they already have grandchildren to look after?

The ages of our parents at death give some guide to our genes, which partly determine the duration of our lives. With reasonable luck in life's lottery we are likely to live a little longer than they, as average longevity steadily rises in the western world. Longevity correlates with walking speed, handgrip, standing balance and ease of rising from a chair. What does that mean in practice? It means that we should take regular brisk walks.

When two measurements do not correlate they do not rise and fall together. So neither thing measured is likely to accentuate the other. If people, who walked faster, did not live longer there would be no point in walking faster to live longer. When measurements correlate they do rise and fall together. But it does not tell us that walking faster will make us live longer. It might just be that those destined for long lives tend to walk faster for entirely different reasons. Only further studies can give us the answer. Meanwhile common sense tells me that walking a lot will make me walk faster, improve my health and probably prolong my life.

Although happy people live longer, unhappy people may cling to life more than happy ones. Happy people are grateful for what they have had and unhappiness does not remove the fear of death.

Eventually we all have to leave the other guests to enjoy the party without us, however much we look after our health. We would like to leave quickly while we are still enjoying the fun but it does not always happen like that. Increasing disability mars the last years of life for some despite all that medicine can do. It is rational to fear the diseases which destroy the quality of life more than those which actually end life. But we are not rational creatures especially when events touch us closely. Nevertheless, as life strips from us the pleasures of our youth, we can savour better those that remain.

If you live long enough you experience everything, well more and more things, and recently I tried a colonoscopy. I will not pain you by describing the procedure, and actually it did not pain me either, because I remember nothing about it. But the purgative preparation was unforgettable.

A decreasing percentage of old people enjoy themselves, as age advances and physical and intellectual powers decline. The test is whether life still has a definitely positive quality. We can be happy in old age and even extreme old age, provided we accept that physical powers decline. What kills it for us is intellectual decline and loss of independence. A friend told me that his ninety-year-old aunt is disappointed when she wakes up each morning. She would have preferred an eternal to a temporary sleep. Will our grandchildren be considering voluntary euthanasia for those, who just think they have lived too long? It seems horrific now but it may not do so fifty years from now.

Medicated survival

Medical advances have prolonged our lives (and clean water and good food have done so even more). Progress always brings problems and we go on living now when life is making neither us nor anyone else happy. In the past it was the doctor's duty to do everything possible to prolong life. Everything has not been very much throughout human history, because medicine was an art, not a science. It was also good sense, compassion, an unjustified air of competence, and willingness to take the responsibility from the patient and the family. That is no light matter, if the patient is a gangster's daughter. A shrewd ancient Egyptian medical text advised doctors to refuse to treat some conditions, because there was no honour to be gained from doing so. But honour is providing comfort when there is no cure.

Doctors now have moral problems unknown in former times. They often have to decide when to switch from delaying death to easing it and they are tempted to wait too long. In the UK nearly 60% of us die in an acute hospital, mostly without wanting to. (I mean die in the hospital, not die.) The doctors there are programmed to make patients better and get them home quickly both to release the bed for the next patient and because the sooner we leave the better for us. Hospitals must be dangerous places, if most of us die there. They are full of harmful bugs, resistant to antibiotics. What the doctors are not so good at is easing up and easing the death of a patient, who is never going home. Modern techniques, such as ventilators and artificial kidneys, make us ask whether someone, who could be kept alive, should be kept alive. Doctors do not like defeat and it is the duty of relatives sometimes to tell them to give in. If life is neither useful nor happy, we confer no benefit by prolonging it.

> I was called to see a man with a very high blood potassium level. He was totally paralysed and his heart was weak. Swiftly I injected an antidote into his vein and set up the necessary infusion. I stood back satisfied as his heart strengthened and he sat up. Then, with the doctor temporarily covering the ward, I looked at his notes and saw that he had terminal cancer with a few more miserable days to go.

You can't do the right thing without knowing all the facts. But perhaps he wanted those extra few days. Stupid decisions can prove to be good ones. And when we act for the best it does not always turn out for the best.

There are two countries, which do not believe in death. In Greece the State continues to pay some citizens their pensions after they have died. In the US they tend to regard death as a failure of medical treatment, not a necessary part of life. The US spends much of its enormous health budget on people in the last year of their lives. Therefore all that effort cannot be doing people much good. Infant mortality rates are not wonderful there and average longevity is two years less than in the UK. Those are good indicators of the overall health of a nation. It is less how much you spend than how you spend it.

There is a divergence of religious practice regarding the prolongation of life. Islamic and orthodox Jewish traditions cling to the idea that doctors should prolong it, whenever possible. Only God has the right to terminate their efforts. However, unwise attempts to prolong life may be harmful and contrary to the patient's likely wishes. Doctors can sometimes try too hard.

> A distinguished scientist was kept alive long after he should have been allowed to die with dignity. Everything was done for him, including inappropriate brain surgery, resulting in permanent coma, when he would probably have preferred death.

Doctors should not act in ways they see as harmful to their patients even on request. But they should not try to stop another doctor complying with the request, if he takes a different view.

> A Muslim man had heart failure, multiple strokes, and widespread vascular disease. His life was wrecked but he was most immediately dying of renal failure. His family insisted that his life should be prolonged by dialysis. I thought that a brief prolongation of misery was not in his best interest.

Christian attitudes can be more realistic about attempts to prolong life. And duties to our family and society do not stop until we are dead. When we want enormously expensive treatment, which will benefit us very little, we should remember that we might deprive others of treatment, which would benefit them much.

It is permitted with the patient's consent, to interrupt advanced medical techniques, where the results fall short of expectations…. one cannot impose on anyone the obligation to have recourse to a technique which is burdensome….. Such a refusal should be considered as an acceptance of the human condition, or a wish to avoid the application of a medical procedure disproportionate to the results that can be expected, or a desire not to impose excessive expense on the family or the community. [2]

To avoid these problems it is possible to write a living will, which is a strange expression, because you can hardly write a will, when you are dead. It is an advance directive about your medical treatment, if you become unable to indicate your wishes. It can tell doctors not to prolong your life by certain means in certain circumstances, when you are no longer competent to refuse consent to treatment. The problem is that it is hard to foresee exact circumstances, both your own and those of medical science. Nevertheless, it can give a clear indication of your attitude to your doctor and your family. The sensible instruction is that you want your doctors to use their good sense to refrain from treatment, which would prolong life without quality.

Some people do not give up the struggle, even when they are dead. In the US there are some cryopreservation enthusiasts. They hope to be revived from the freezer, when medicine has advanced enough to cure, what it cannot cure today. They are incurable optimists as well as incurable patients. Current technology is not able to preserve them in a condition, from which they might be successfully revived. They are also incurable egoists. With their family and friends long gone, who will want them in some future time? Their fate will be hygienic disposal, not revival.

5

Feeling More Peaceful About Dying

The great thing about death is that you do not have to pack. But life actually is like packing for a holiday. You always put the wrong things into the suitcase and leave out the right ones and that is just what we do with our lives. You make more mistakes about packing when visiting somewhere new and this is our first visit to this Earth. It is probably also our last.

With a holiday you can hope to enjoy it. With death you pay for the refreshments after the funeral but never get to taste them. Some anticipate happiness after death but the chances of fun on holiday are probably better.

Fear of death

It is natural to fear death. We are so afraid of it that we comfort ourselves with thoughts of a life after death. How long would we live, if we were not afraid of death? A species, which stopped making vigorous efforts to avoid it, would not survive long

It is irrational to fear the eternity after we have gone, but show total nonchalance about the eternity before we came. Instinct trumps rationality. Epicurus (341-271 BC), who was not actually such an epicurean, did not believe in a life after this one. [1] Nevertheless he advised us not to fear death. He taught that life was a series of sense experiences, and since there are no sense experiences after life ends, there is no reason to fear death. Anyone, who has been anaesthetised will remember being wheeled into the anteroom to the theatre, and will next remember waking up back in bed. I suppose death is the same except that you do not wake up, although you will never know that you did not.

Death is a natural part of the cycle of our lives. Doctors sometimes find this easier to accept personally than professionally. Their training inevitably has such an emphasis on cure. As death draws near we worry about what is happening to us but also about being a burden to our families and not being able to care for our loved ones. It is strange that the young are more careless of their lives than the old, who have less to lose. But the old have lost that attribute of youth, a sense of invulnerability.

We are a fairly long lived species. Perhaps humans tend to survive to be grandparents because they share in the rearing of the young. Grandmothers usually do more than grandfathers so nature sensibly allows women to live longer than men. Childcare is a useful occupation for widowed granny.

Many invertebrates die after reproduction because they are no longer necessary, if they do not rear the young. There could hardly be a species with a tendency to die before reproduction. Some female spiders carry the process to its logical conclusion by making a satisfying meal out of the male after coition. No doubt some human males think that they made the same mistake as the male spider but when the penis erects by trapping blood, it also traps good sense.

Species do not survive forever. Crocodiles have lasted more than a hundred million years. Their design must have been fit for purpose. Mammalian species last about a million years on average. Neanderthal man survived only half a million years before we displaced him. Homo sapiens has so far lasted two hundred thousand years. Few would gamble on us outlasting the Neanderthals. Technological advance will deliver increasingly powerful weapons to an increasing number of fanatics, who will be happy to destroy themselves, if by doing so they can destroy the rest of us. We must take precautions without letting fear damage our lives.

Preparation for death

We have no duties after death, because there is no action that we can take. But when we get older we should turn our minds to the future interests of others after we are dead. There are three matters which must be discussed frankly with appropriate members of our family despite our embarrassment; they are sex, money and death. You can find all you need to know about sex in the magazines in the hairdressing salon and also some things you never wanted to know. I will deal with money and death. If you don't discuss death together while you are well, will you raise the funeral arrangements for the first time with your dying spouse?

Do not make unreasonable deathbed requests of your nearest and dearest or harbour unreasonable expectations of them. Graves and memorials may be a comfort to survivors but grandchildren are unlikely to visit them and their children will not even know where they are. And they will be just as uninterested in urns with our ashes. Cremation and appropriate dispersal of the ashes seems final and hygienic but wastes fossil fuel. Ecological burial in a cardboard box is more virtuous, although it is still less usual. There is one thing we should try to persuade our family to do. Agree that our organs should bring life to others when they are no longer of any use to us.

We may hope for sudden, unexpected death in happy old age, whether on the golf course or during sleep. But it is an ambition which involves a failure of responsibility. The dying have duties, which differ from those of the well, but are nevertheless important. Sudden death denies family and friends the chance to take their leave. It means that unfinished business will remain forever unfinished. There can be no reconciliation with the sister, from whom you cut yourself off thirty years ago, because she persuaded your mother to leave a few pounds more to her than to you. Worse still it prevents reconciliation with the child, whom you cut off, because she married for love and not to please you.

Preparation for bereavement

She first deceased. He for a little tried
To live without her. Liked it not and died.

When we live most of our lives with one partner, it is difficult to live on without him or her. Long-term partners tend to specialise in different household duties. Even today the man often organises the finances and the woman is in sole charge of the cleaning and the cooking. Whoever is left does not know how to do the other jobs. The last thing we need on bereavement is the added stress of being lost dealing with matters we do not understand.

We should prepare for bereavement. A man should learn how to clean a house and cook simple meals. A woman should practise paying the bills and dealing with the banks. Both names should be registered with banks, service companies and insurance companies so that they recognise the surviving partner. Each partner should leave the other a folder of simple instructions. It can be useful to register lasting powers of attorney. Doing so is tedious and expensive but probably worth it. Each partner needs to know how much income he or she will have after the death of the other. Pensions can be reduced or lost. We need to discuss with each other where the survivor should live and when to move.

After bereavement do not make major decisions too soon. Give time for grief and express your grief. Try to stay active. Remember the one who has gone, would want you to continue to enjoy life. To do so is to fulfil their wishes.

Finding a new companion is a good idea but be cautious about moving in together. Sort out the financial arrangements and the family visiting rota first. Her grandchildren are high spirited and delightful. His are badly brought up. If you do move in together, do not give up your own home immediately, because it may not work out.

When dealing with the bereaved just listen to them. Widows can become non-persons. People try to avoid them in the street and shun them at parties. They are so afraid of saying the wrong thing that they do the worst thing of all and ignore them. Widowers have the relative advantage of scarcity value and the disadvantage of being lost with household mechanics. Some widows need a handyman for simple do-it-yourself jobs.

Where to die

My mother quarrelled with her elder sister about who should have the honour of looking after my paralysed grandmother. My aunt was deeply hurt, when grandma died in our house, during the time that she spent with us, because that honour should have gone to her. Today they would probably have put her in a nursing home, although many still sacrifice their lives as unsung carers.

We have an ancestral memory of dying in our own bed surrounded by grieving relatives, consoled by the thought that we will be winging to paradise, and leaving behind some nice bequests. Times have changed and sadly many of us die in an acute hospital, as failures of modern medical care, although we would prefer to die at home. It is better to die in a hospice, where the staff try to ease death, not prolong life. Hospices are so good at symptom control, because the doctors and the nurses know that they are there for that purpose. They know that their patients should take each day at a time, and glean from it whatever good there is in it. Some of us die at home with our symptoms relieved by skilled nurses, advised by doctors increasingly aware of the importance of terminal care. We always need the right person for the problem, be it doctor, solicitor, accountant, barber or spouse.

When are you dead?

Obsessive fear about being buried alive was common in Victorian times as exemplified by the Edgar Allan Poe story, *The Fall of the House of Usher*. There were horror stories of scratches found on the inside of coffin lids. Some people arranged to be buried with alarms in their coffins, just in case they woke up. Humphry Davy, the distinguished scientist, who discovered electrolysis and invented the miners' safety lamp, requested a delay of ten days between his death and his burial in 1829 to avoid any mistake.

It certainly is possible to make a mistaken diagnosis of death. Before certifying death I usually looked at the back of the eye through an ophthalmoscope because interruption of the column of blood in the retinal vessels proved conclusively that the circulation had stopped. There are stories of breathing being noticed by mortuary attendants but I do not think that anyone has revived for more than a brief period. Rare it is to return to consciousness in a refrigerator in the morgue or in the cold ground. If you have any worries about it, then choose cremation, because not even Houdini could emerge alive from the crematorium chimney.

There are good practical and moral reasons for knowing with certainty, who is dead and, who is not, especially in these days of organ donation. The one thing that all agree about death is its irreversibility. No one comes back. A body cell dies, when its organised activity stops irreversibly. If it can be restarted then the cell was not dead. The same applies to an organ like the brain or the heart and also to the whole person. If a person is dead, he cannot be brought back to life; if he can, he was not dead.

People talk a lot of nonsense about near death experiences. Near death is totally different from actual death. The confusion arises, because the words near and nearly have two distinct meanings. If I am nearly six feet tall, then I am very similar to people, who are actually six feet tall. We are describing a minor quantitative difference. If I nearly fell out of a high window, then I still belong among those, who have not fallen out of high windows, and very definitely not with those, who have suffered that misfortune. Nearly, in the latter case, indicates that a major qualitative change almost took place but never did and I have remained the same. I have nothing in common with those who have fallen out of high windows. Similarly those, who experience near death, have nothing in common with those who have died.

They may have strange sensations and psychic experiences during resuscitation, but all the time they have remained firmly anchored to their beds in varying degrees of unconsciousness and cerebral anoxia. There are natural explanations for the phenomena, which they describe. They were not dead, because they recovered, and they can tell us nothing about being dead.

The modern dispute about diagnosing death is whether you are dead, when your heart still beats, but brain function has irreversibly gone. Some countries only recognise death after the heart has stopped beating. Japan is an example. This is a question of some importance, partly to avoid the misuse of scarce intensive care facilities, and partly because organs for donation stay in better condition when they are taken from beating heart donors.

The introduction of ventilators has caused the problem. Breathing requires an intact breathing centre in the brain stem, but the heart beats automatically, even if the brain is dead. Formerly when respiration stopped, the heart stopped a few minutes later, because of oxygen lack. If the patient is ventilated, the heart may continue to beat, even though the brain is dead. The person may be pink and look very much alive to the family. It distresses them to be told he is dead but when our brains are dead so are we.

Look at it this way. Jones goes into hospital with heart failure and Smith goes into hospital with a fatal head injury. When Smith dies his wife generously allows his heart to be transplanted into Jones. The rest of Smith now goes to the crematorium, but Jones goes home to a rejoicing Mrs Jones, with Smith's heart inside him and his own heart discarded. Now Mrs Jones thinks that she has recovered her husband completely. She does not think that a Mr Jones-Smith has returned to her. Mrs Smith thinks that her husband is quite dead. She is happy for Mr and Mrs Jones and is pleased she made the gift, because something good has come out of her sorrow. But she does not believe that Mr Jones partly belongs to her, and should live with her one day each month. Clearly both ladies think that our essence is in our brains, not our hearts.

Suicide

Can it ever be right to kill yourself? To many religions life is a gift from God and it is his right alone to take it back. It is certainly impolite to return unwanted gifts to a disappointed donor. So we must respect our own lives as well as those of other people. But if God has allowed your life to become so awful that you want to end it, what started as a gift has become an imposition.

For some religions there is another problem. Suicide is the one sin, which by definition no one can repent, unless you take a slow acting, irreversible poison, like paraquat. If a mortal sin, like murdering yourself, is not repented, the gates of Hell open.

Certainly suicide cannot always be wrong. Surely it is right to kill yourself to avoid betraying friends under torture. No principle can be so absolute that it always overrules every other principle in all situations. Here the duty not to harm friends is more important than the duty not to kill yourself.

In usual circumstances the situation likely to face the older person is a deteriorating quality of life through fatal illness or increasing dependency. You hope that death is not far away but wish it were nearer. You have accomplished all that you ever will; you are in distress and your distress is aggravated by what your suffering is doing to your loved ones. There is no disrespect for the law, in jurisdictions, where suicide is no longer a crime. It is difficult to see why suicide is necessarily wrong when there is no prospect of future happiness.

What are the arguments against it? First you must be sure that you are not seeing everything too black because you are in the grip of a depression, which might respond to treatment. Your family and friends may be distressed at your unexpected departure. They may wonder whether they might have done more for you; they may regret leaving certain words unspoken and actions not taken. It is best to have the reluctant acquiescence of those nearest to you. They should want to see your suffering end and respect your wishes. The note, which you leave behind, may not be sufficient.

The morality of suicide becomes a balance between the cost to oneself of refraining from it and the cost to others of proceeding. Some may think that that the cost of refraining can be too high. Others may think that respect for the sanctity of life overrides all other considerations. No one should want to impose his morality on another person, except to protect a third person.

> The Samaritans are volunteers, who offer counselling by telephone to those in despair and often contemplating suicide. One told me that when she hears some of their stories her unspoken thought is occasionally that suicide is their best option. She never voices it. An elderly Samaritan in a nearby town unexpectedly killed himself. Doctors are reluctant to consult their colleagues about mental health problems. Did similar reasons inhibit him from talking to his colleagues?

A competent person may commit passive suicide by refusing life -prolonging treatment, such as ventilation or dialysis. It is disrespect to his autonomy to impose or continue that treatment. A court might be right to overrule him under three conditions. The treatment would be clearly beneficial; there is at least a little doubt about his competence; there is reason to believe he might later change his mind. If he is never going to want to stay alive, how can keeping him alive be a benefit?

What to leave behind

It is a truism that the best things to leave behind you are fond memories, a good name, and no debts. The money which you leave, may not do all that much good to those you love. Most have a strong aversion to leaving it to the Chancellor but it may do least harm in his possession. All he can do is waste it. Where there's a Will there's a quarrel and where there isn't, there's a bigger quarrel. Fights between siblings over Wills are frequent and fierce. A bank manager said that he had seen fisticuffs in his office over the Will. I suspect that it is not always the money and the heirlooms themselves, which cause such bitter quarrels, but what they represent in terms of parental love and the performance of filial duty. Therefore rich offspring usually want equal shares with their poorer siblings. The daughter with three children thinks she needs the money for them and the daughter with none thinks that she should have the money as compensation. The simple rule is to divide the money equally.

There is also a strong case for giving it to your heirs with a warm hand not a cold hand. You may have some influence on how they spend it while you are alive and you can see them enjoy it. It is more rewarding when they address their gratitude to your ears not your grave.

I offer a word of advice for the wealthy, who are also people with feelings. Do not resent inheritance tax. It is a wealth tax, which is perhaps fairer than income or purchase tax. Moreover it is a tax on the wealth of your heirs, who did not work for the money. Your responsibilities are to see that your children do not spend their old age in poverty and that your grandchildren get a good education and do not finish their education in deep debt. It is bad for them to have sums of money to waste. It removes the incentive to struggle, and they will probably spend it in ways, which will harm them. They buy fast cars, which they are not competent to drive. Even the prospect of money is dangerous, as they can take out loans in anticipation.

A friend sent his child to college reasonably financed. Unsurprisingly she promptly went into substantial debt. He wrote to the bank demanding that senior management explain why the bank lent money to an eighteen year old away from home for the first time, when they knew she started the term adequately funded. The response from high up came. "If we did not lend the money to your child, other banks would." The high street banks are simply businesses until they need charity from the taxpayer.

The life after this one

Philosophy should comfort us when we contemplate death. If there were no deaths, life would seem an eternity and there would be no room for new lives. But I think that more writers advise comfort from philosophy than readers derive it. Religion is a more effective source of comfort. It would be nice to think there was a life after this one, in which our true worth would be appreciated, and our enemies obliged to acknowledge it.

There are problems with the concept of an afterlife. We have no real evidence that there is one. Can mind or soul survive without brain? Nobody comes back to tell us. As Shakespeare's Hamlet elegantly expressed the commonplace thought, it is "the undiscover'd country, from whose bourn no traveller returns." [2] But Hamlet had just spoken with his father's ghost, hot from purgatory, so worrying over his instructions must have made him forget the encounter.

Moreover religions do not agree on the nature of an afterlife. Orthodox Judaism offers bodily resurrection, to the extent of formally burying amputated limbs. Hinduism rewards the good with a superior life in the next incarnation, but without any memory of the virtuous deeds in the preceding life, which gained promotion. In usual Western thought a person must think himself to be the same person at different times and in different places, in order to be the same person. It is difficult to see how the person who does the good deeds is rewarded, if he and the one who enjoys the reward are both unaware of the other's existence. Christianity offers a spiritual bliss in the form of proximity to God. As Christopher Marlowe (1564-93) puts into the mouth of Mephistopheles, when Dr Faustus asks him why he is not in hell.

> Why, this is hell, nor am I out of it.
> Think'st thou that I, who saw the face of God,
> And tasted the eternal joys of heaven,
> Am not tormented with ten thousand hells,
> In being depriv'd of everlasting bliss? [3]

But how should we be more peaceful about dying, if we think that this life is all there is? Well it is foolish to fret about the unavoidable. It is absurd to hope for exemption from the universal. We can look back and be satisfied if we have done a little more good than harm, fulfilled a few duties, despite failing in many, and enjoyed days of modest happiness and moments of great joy. We can look forwards, detached from old struggles and enmities, to perform a few more duties. If we are lucky, we can still take some pleasure in living, and if not, we must hope to sleep soon. We must not dwell on our mistakes, our sins or our missed opportunities. The past is another country and we should visit it only briefly.

Conclusion

Responsibilities never cease. We must fulfil them as we face death and consider how they may best be fulfilled after our deaths. We have led imperfect lives with failures of the will, the judgement, and the heart. Never mind; there are no perfect people. If we kept trying, then we did our duty. Happiness also changes but does not have to disappear on the road to death. And then after life we vanish or sleep at peace in the dust, if you prefer. Or perhaps when our maker asks us searching questions we will be able to put a few to him.

6

Justice Between The Generations

When the ship is going down the cry is "women and children first" but is that both ageist and sexist? And when the snooty assistant told me in the smart outfitters in the local posh town that they did not put small size jumpers in the sale, was that "sizeist"?

Actually the shop was not discriminating against small men; it was unwisely correlating pocket size with body size. It closed a few months later. Saving women in preference to men is unjust discrimination, although most men would be too embarrassed to protest. Giving preference to children over old people is arguably fair discrimination, not prejudice.

Older people are unhappy when we are given inferior treatment. We are less unhappy when such discrimination is based on correct facts and shared values. We should reluctantly accept disadvantageous treatment, if it is justly based. When discrimination is based on incorrect facts old people should not accept it. When there is a clash of values the case must be argued.

There are several types of discrimination based on incorrect facts or the misuse of correct facts. They are varieties of unjust discrimination or prejudice.

I. **It is untrue of the group**. Old people can benefit from many medical procedures, which were once denied to them, because they were wrongly thought to be too dangerous for them.

2. **It is untrue of the person, even if true of the group.** Many nonagenarians might not survive the operation but this tough old body probably would.

3. **It is true of all groups**. Politicians in Africa may often be corrupt but so they are everywhere else.

4. **It is true but irrelevant.** You are old but that has no bearing on your ability to do this particular job.

5. **Groups cannot be fairly compared.** The achievement of persons and groups can be compared fairly, only if circumstances and opportunities are similar. Discovering and nurturing the bright child in the semiliterate family is a public duty.

6. **A defect is emphasised and qualities dismissed.** Even correct and relevant factual statements can constitute prejudice, if they are misleadingly selective. The old man applying for the job may be less receptive to

new ideas but he is likely to be more conscientious and have more experience than the young man.

So is it ever right to treat citizens differently because they are older? I mean just because they are older, not because of any physical or mental decline.

Age and health care rationing

No country can afford state of the art medical treatment in all fields for all citizens. That is no excuse for selectively treating old patients in the oldest wards in the hospital, less well staffed and less pleasant than other wards. John F Kennedy in a message to Congress said that a society's quality and durability can be best measured by the respect and care given to its elderly citizens. [1] Yet the British Medical Journal gives harrowing accounts showing that the NHS is failing elderly patients. [2]

Wards devoted to the care of older people should be pleasanter and better staffed than other wards. The patients stay there longer and need more help with everyday living. Sadly geriatrics is often seen as a "Cinderella" speciality practised in "Cinderella" wards. Most of us can do little about it except protest vigorously at the treatment of our relatives because we will be too weak to protest at our own treatment when our turn comes.

But there is another side to this story. It faces us less often but it is still important both in principle and in practice. The rationing of lifesaving health care is sometimes unavoidable. Its availability may be limited; supply cannot meet need, as with donor organs or powerful new drugs, such as insulin or penicillin, which are scarce at first. Choosing whom to save is unavoidable. In these situations is it right to discriminate against the old simply because they are old?

You may be surprised to know that in those circumstances I think that discrimination on grounds of age alone is just. I put this forward in learned journals and was attacked by The President of the Royal College of Physicians and a minister of health among many others. [3] A distinguished geriatrician tried to get my health authority to take action against me. I was sadly incorrect politically and some told me that they agreed with me but would not be so stupid as to say so publicly. But the dogmas of political correctness change more rapidly than those of religion. The British Medical Journal followed the party line at the time but was happy to publish the following recently.

> The ethically and scientifically most unacceptable aspect of management by absolute risk is the ignoring of the relative importance of loss of life at different ages. No modern society with a low risk of mortality places equal value on a death at age 45 and one at age 75.

It is strange how wicked proposals can become received wisdom so quickly. But we are interested in what actually is right or wrong, not in the orthodoxy of the moment. And if we are unlucky enough to be denied such care one day so that a younger person can have it, should we rage against the injustice or accept the decision with as good grace as possible? We all hope to be elderly one day and more and more of us already are. Think of the alternative. As such we want the working population to do what is right by us but we should not want more. We want all the medical care from which we can benefit. But if it is necessary to choose between the life of a young person and that of an old person, how should society decide?

I set out my stall again. The proposition is that, when life-saving health care is rationed, we must take account of large differences in age, and favour the younger person. The doctor should do this and as older patients we should accept it. The anti-ageist claim is simply that age is an irrelevant criterion when we are obliged to choose who to save and who not to save. Some other criterion must be used.

First what is our intuition about it? Let us discover whether or not you are an ageist. Would you save the life of a thirty-year-old or a seventy-year-old, everything else being equal?

> There is an epidemic of myocarditis, causing fatal heart failure. On the same day two patients with rapidly failing hearts are admitted to the hospital. They are otherwise healthy and both would make a good recovery after a heart transplant. One is aged thirty and one is aged seventy. A single donor heart equally compatible with both becomes available. Who should have it? If you would give it to the younger person, then you are an ageist. If you would spin a coin to decide, then you are not.

Try a second thought experiment.

> You have two dogs, equally loved, one aged fifteen years and one aged two years. They have the same illness, which it will cost a fortune to treat, and you have only one fortune. How will you decide which to treat, and which to put down?

In Russian folk tales, when the wolves are gaining on the sledge, it is always grandpa, who jumps off, to speed the sledge and delay the wolves, while they eat him. We older people have always individually put the lives of our children first. If not, we should do. It is logical that collectively we should do the same. I might not want to die for your grandchildren but I would agree to die with you to save all our grandchildren. I would not be happy about making the sacrifice but I would be content that it was a duty or at least I should be.

I found that everyone gave me the ageist answer, when I asked these questions privately. Perhaps they knew the answer I wanted. But in 1995 it was politically incorrect to go public. However, even if our intuition is ageist, the intuition must be backed by correct facts and shared values.

The utilitarian argument is that saving the life of a young person saves more life years than saving the life of an old person. Utilitarianism tells us to increase happiness in the world. Saving young persons adds more happiness than saving old persons because they will gain more years to be happy. If we are unable to do all the good we want to do, it is logical to do as much good as we can.

The egalitarian argument is that it is fairer to add ten years to the life of a twenty-year-old than ten years to the life of an eighty-year-old. The old person has already had a fair innings but the young person has not. Distributive justice demands a degree of equalisation.

Now let us look at the arguments put forward against ageism.

- Rationing of health care is immoral. The dilemma is therefore false.

So I have to repeat the facts. Some treatments have to be rationed for the reasons given above. For utilitarian and egalitarian reasons age offers a just rationing criterion.

The need for the rationing of medical care will increase. Medical care is increasingly sophisticated and the population steadily ages and needs more care so costs will always increase. Sadly the cheapest patient is the dead one. I am not talking about hip or cataract operations, which Britain is rich enough to provide for all its citizens. But some new drugs, for example chemotherapy, are prohibitively expensive and offer only limited prolongation of life compared to cheaper alternatives. If the NHS pays for them others will go without treatment. You cannot spend the same penny twice. Would not the effort be better put into the early diagnosis and cure of cancer? A visceral distaste for any rationing of health care can lead to refusal to face reality.

- Discriminating against the old is as wrong as discriminating against people because they are black.

If that were true it would be Type 1 discrimination. It is not true, because those born black stay black. We are all born young and become old, if we are lucky. So growing old is the fate of us all, at least the fortunate ones; the old are not a separate group.

- Chronological age does not always reflect biological age.

One man is biologically ten years older than another man of the same age. So favouring the younger person can be Type 2 discrimination. First, that objection is irrelevant to the egalitarian argument. Second, it is wrong to exaggerate your opponent's argument. We are only considering really large differences in chronological age, which are likely to outweigh biological factors. Women live longer than men but they should not have preferential treatment. They live only about four years longer; that is enough to put a premium on old men in the dating game but not enough to give women preference for lifesaving treatment.

- We value people of all ages equally, because we punish the killing of an old person as severely as the killing of a young person.

That is rightly so, because punishment is directed at the criminal, not his victim. All the victims are humans and the law does not concern itself with their characteristics or qualities. We award the same size medal to one who saves an old person, as to one who saves a young person. Again we are concerned with the valour and public spirit of the rescuer, to which the age of the person rescued is irrelevant.

- The old person may be a wonderful man, who has served humanity, and the young man may be fairly useless.

The argument is that ageism is Type 6 discrimination. But it would be appalling, if doctors took it upon themselves to assess the moral worth of their patients and prioritise treatment according to their personal opinions.

The utilitarian principle may sometimes make saving the older life more important. Age is far from the sole rationing criterion. If a young person will not cooperate with treatment, more years of life will be gained by treating an older person. Also I am discussing the situation in developed countries. To some African tribes the lives of the old may be more important than those of the young, because of their accumulated wisdom. The old elephant cow is more important than the calf, because she can lead the herd to the water holes. Here discrimination is just because it is based on fact not prejudice.

So it is our duty as older people in the western world reluctantly to accept the occasional "ageist" decision, if we are unlucky enough to meet it.

Age and medical research

Medical research is often unjust to older people. Drug trials do not usually recruit patients over the age of 70 years. So we older people do not know whether the results of the trial apply to us. More of such trials should be directed towards older people. To give myself a puff, I published a study of a method of measuring urinary protein excretion and followed it up by another study showing that the method also worked for older patients. [4]

On the other hand I doubt the wisdom of basic biological research aimed at a major prolongation of our lives. There was a vigorous e-mail controversy in the Journal of Medical Ethics about the desirability of increasing the pace of research into the ageing process. [5] Most contributors thought it was a wonderful idea, obviously relishing the prospect of living long into a second century. They were libertarians and thought that people should live as long as they wanted to live. I was a communitarian and thought that we ought to consider whether it would be good for humanity in general, if people started to live so long.

They were idealists and thought it was a crying shame to lose eighty-year-old parents. I was a cynic and was appalled at the idea of not losing them. I have seen frail seventy-year-old ladies shamelessly bullied by peppery ninety-year-old mothers. Some older women feel torn in two by the conflicting demands of aged parents and little grandchildren. We will find it difficult to refuse the new elixir of life but will we be happier, when we all live longer?

Years ago the man from the British Medical Association told me not to worry about my pension after seventy because I would not be able to spend any money anyway. But now they predict that one in six of us will reach our century. Why spend resources trying to improve what is already improving? Why make a situation worse, when it is already causing problems? Who will pay for our pensions when the old so much outnumber the young? What if it means that more and more of us suffer from senile dementia? The problem with the prolongation of life which we have achieved so far, is that the period of decline also prolongs. I doubt that the scientists will enable us to live for two hundred years and then suddenly go out like an electric lamp. Will we be obliged not just to permit assisted suicide but to enforce it? There is a time to live and a time to die.

There are already rather too many of us for the planet to hold. We are polluting the land, the sea and the air. The fish will disappear and the land will overheat. Animals fight when they are kept in cages, which are too crowded, and humans will fight for water and other limited resources. If living longer is not going to overcrowd the planet, then clearly fewer children must be born. The problems associated with the compulsory limitation of family size have been seen in China.

Nevertheless I admit that the battle is already lost. Research will one day make it possible to prolong human life well beyond a century. Indeed scientific advances in this field are frequent. The money will anyway always be in research to gratify the desires of the rich, not the needs of the poor. The disparity between the duration of life in poor and rich countries will increase, bringing more injustice into an unjust world. The discrimination will be between the rich and the poor, not between old and young. Scientists working in this field should be supported in more useful research.

When we have had a fair innings, there is a responsibility to give others a turn with the bat. Even if you agree with me, what can you do about it as an individual? The short answer is not a lot. I certainly would not ask you not to prolong your life, if you can. But what we really want is to prolong our health, not our lives.

Justice and jobs

Older women television presenters feel that they are elbowed out in favour of younger eye candy. That is probably true but it is not necessarily unfair discrimination. Both old and young prefer young and attractive presenters, with exceptions made for much loved older ones. Commercial television stations are businesses, which must attract an audience to earn advertising revenue. Viewers have choice and vote with their remote controls. The use of younger presenters is a commercial necessity. Even the BBC, although it has non-commercial responsibilities, must consider viewing figures. Second, if you get the job over other candidates because you are young and pretty, it is hypocritical to complain about losing it when you no longer are. Live by the sword and die by the sword.

When someone over fifty loses a job it may be hard to find another. Employers seem to prefer younger workers. Often they feel they can pay them less and they adapt better to new practices. But young people may be less conscientious than older employees. Older people are less likely to skive from work or suffer hangovers, and they turn up even when they feel poorly. Naturally these are generalisations. I admired some young nurses, who trudged for two hours through thick snow to reach work on time. But sometimes generalisations are unavoidable, even though they can involve making errors of Type 2.

In the interest of our society it is far more important that the young work than the old. It is more important that the father of a family works than that his elderly father should, however beneficial it is to grandpa to keep occupied. Unemployed people become depressed and lose self-respect. They cannot set an example of regular work to their children. If young people do not have to get out of bed early each morning to go to work by the time they are in their mid-twenties, It becomes something which they will never do Some unemployed young men turn to crime. Aimless young women may have babies and then find out that caring for them is a drag. When we older people are denied work we certainly have problems both financial and psychological. But we do not turn to drugs, pregnancy or burglary. There is a social duty to see that the young receive a good education and after it start work. Much as you might want to work it is more important that your grandson does. Abolishing the compulsory retirement age in the UK has been a socially retrograde step.

The UK discourages young people from going to university by charging heavy fees, which will leave them with large debts. Hundreds of thousands of children grow up in poverty. Meanwhile in the UK wealthy pensioners receive untaxed heating allowances, free television licences, pay no prescription charges and have free bus passes. Yet the future of the country lies in the nurture of the young. At the least such benefits should be taxed and the proceeds used to support our children. This will not happen because the number of pensioners increases and we are more likely to vote than the young.

In these respects we are unjust to the young. It might not make us happy to see preference given to them but sometimes we should accept that it is just, which will make us slightly less unhappy. There is injustice between the generations in both directions. Only political action can remedy it and that is beyond my scope.

7

Why Does Making Other People Happy Make Us Happy?

At least it makes most of us happy. Like our overall feeling of happiness the specific pleasure we take in making others happy is partly pre-set but fluctuates both spontaneously and in response to thoughts and events. The nicest of us are not always nice. But why is there this almost universal pleasure in helping others? It can cost us time, effort or money. So why are we happy when we do it and unhappy when we don't?

Sympathy or reason

David Hume (1711-76) thought that emotions, such as benevolence and sympathy, make us perform good actions. He considered that reason could only show us how to go about doing them, not make us do them.

But Immanuel Kant thought that morality could only be derived from a sense of duty dictated by our rational minds. He thought that an action could not be good if you did it just because you enjoyed it. Although he did accept that doing your duty could make you happy. "Reason must have the capacity to induce a feeling of pleasure or of delight in the fulfilment of duty."

He had four objections to Hume's claim that sympathy, not reason, is the source of goodness to others. None of them are convincing.

- Sentiment is not binding, unlike duty. But should we not do what our hearts tell us, as well as our heads?
- Feelings can move you to vice as well as virtue. And so can a misplaced sense of duty, as totalitarian states have shown.
- We do not all have the same strength of feeling. And the strength of the sense of duty also varies from person to person.
- Reason is necessary to control our actions, however well intentioned. That is common ground to both Kant and Hume.

The simple synthesis of the two approaches is that both make us perform good actions. Sometimes we take pleasure in doing good and sometimes we do it because we feel we ought. But insofar as we are unhappy when we fail to do our duty, then Kant and Hume are just describing different sides of the same coin. We are happy when we help and unhappy when we don't.

However, Kant was right that we can't make ourselves have kindly feelings but we can make ourselves act in a kindly way, even without the feelings. Actions unlike feelings are under our control so we can act out of duty without sympathy. We must do our duty, even when it does not make us happy. As George Bernard Shaw says in *Pygmalion*, we have to look after the undeserving as well as the deserving poor, even though it will make us less happy.

Both emotion and a sense of duty contribute to good actions to a varying degree in different people and in the same person at different times. Fortunately love and duty often combine, as when grandparents care for their grandchildren. I incline to the view that good actions spring more often from emotion than from reason. Happiness is an emotion not a rational conclusion and happiness makes us nicer.

There is evidence that our decisions are often made emotionally in the unconscious mind and then rationalised by the conscious mind. Damage to the frontal lobes just above the eye sockets reduces emotions and makes all decisions harder, including moral decisions. Also Kant conceded that: "Providence has provided us with feelings to compensate for the weakness of human nature. Appropriate feelings can motivate those who lack explicit principles." For most of us warm compassion is a more certain source of goodness than cold reason.

Also we ordinary mortals are much more successful at doing good, when we actually enjoy the action itself. Natural inclination increases the ease and the skill with which we act. It increases the pleasure in the action, the responsibility to act, the likelihood that we will act, and our persistence in action. It certainly is easier to keep on doing the right thing when we take pleasure in both the process and the results.

> The novelist Margaret Forster describes how she de-clined to take over the hospital tea round, which her mother had done for years, because she would only have done it out of cold duty. [1] No doubt the patients enjoyed the cheery gossip as much as the tea. It was better to leave the work to a more suited successor, who would do it better, because she enjoyed it more.

A good person performs beneficial actions because he wants to do them. He may enjoy doing them, or feel guilt when he fails to do them; he may make an intellectual decision to do them, or act impulsively out of sympathy. He may follow local tradition or continue a personal habit. Why should it matter? Motives are often mixed and we do not need to know exactly why we help or are helped. Whether we act out of sympathy or duty we feel better inside ourselves for doing it.

Kant thought that we did not act autonomously when we acted out of sympathy or desire because we do not choose our sympathies and desires. But Kant is partly wrong. I do not choose to want the bun but I do choose whether to buy it or keep my penny so I am still autonomous. Autonomy depends on having the penny. So both happiness and autonomy are greatly dependent on the economy. Come back Karl Marx; all is forgiven.

Empathy and sympathy

Empathy is identifying mentally with and understanding another's distress. Sympathy is actually feeling some of his distress. Either or both together can move us to goodness. They usually do go together, as when men cross their legs in the cinema at the sight of the circular saw advancing up James Bond's trouser legs. However, they can be dissociated. We know what it feels like to lose but pleasure at winning leaves little room for sympathy with the loser. Neither he nor we know why the little boy sobs but it still touches the heart. However, it is easier to put oneself out for someone, when we both understand what he is going through and are emotionally moved by it.

If you really can feel emotionally what a particular form of suffering is like, you are less likely to inflict it on others. There is a physiological basis to empathy and sympathy, because, when we see something happen to another person, the same areas of our brains light up as theirs. [2] They say that doctors should suffer some of the humiliations and discomforts to which they submit patients. It will happen to them, but usually after they have stopped treating patients. On the other hand, although we like to think that bullies are cowards, who do not understand what they are doing, it is not true. They are not always cowards and they relish the distress they are causing.

We can probe deeper and ask why we feel sympathy and why do we have a sense of duty.

Heredity

Darwin summarised the development of morality thus.

> The following proposition seems to me in a high degree probable – namely that any animal whatsoever, endowed with well-marked social instincts…. would inevitably acquire a moral sense or conscience, as soon as its intellectual powers had become as well, or nearly as well developed, as in man. [3]

There are many instances of mammals, especially primates, acting in ways which suggest a primitive moral sense. Reciprocity is common. Chimpanzees share food in return for grooming, for support in power struggles and for sex. They show sympathy. They comfort other chimpanzees and humans in distress. They have empathy. Both rats and monkeys may refuse to operate a lever to obtain food, if it causes another rat or monkey to get an electric shock. If they have personally experienced a shock they are more reluctant to inflict it on another. They feel moral closeness. Monkeys are more reluctant to cause a cage mate to receive a shock than a strange monkey. They can be altruistic. Monkeys will help other monkeys to obtain food, even when they do not benefit themselves. Morality is in our blood. The big difference between other animals and us is that we do not just have moral emotions; we can think about moral action.

Animals are programmed to help their kin. It is an ancient biological imperative.

Even some fish guard their own eggs. There are good reasons why genes promoting care of kin should be widely prevalent. The closer your kin the more genes they share with you, and the more likely they are to have caring genes if you have them yourself. Those, who are cared for, are more likely to survive to reproduce. Hence caring genes spread through the population. This applies to humans.

> The biologist J B S Haldane was asked in a pub if he would give up his life for his brother. He answered that he would not, but he would do so for three brothers or nine cousins. [4] His reasoning was that we share half our genes with a brother and one eighth with a cousin, therefore three brothers or nine cousins would pass on more of his own genes than he could.

Darwin realised that this is a cause of altruism among the small groups in which our species has lived for most of its journey. As the members of a small group are dependent on each other, caring spreads beyond immediate kin to community. And when young primates join other groups, as humans may do in marriage, they take with them their caring genes.

Of course evolution never worked by conscious choice until modern man took a hand. We have bred animals selectively for a long time. We choose our mates partly with progeny in mind. Modern societies have even forcibly sterilised women thought to be poor breeding stock. Now there is the possibility of genetic manipulation *in vitro*.

Training

Moral behaviour is instilled in us from infancy. Learned rules of behaviour become innate and unconscious. Both humans and elephants have long lives and a long period of immaturity and dependency. It is essential to their social and moral development that they bond in early life to a carer. Elephants who lose their carer early become aggressive. Monkey mothers may reject their babies, if they have not seen how other monkey mothers care for theirs. Human babies, who have no primary carer in early infancy, may become maladjusted adults. What we see as children affects what we do as adults. Wife beaters have seen their fathers do the same. Decline in the behaviour of children in schools may be due to a decline in active parenting. Criminals often come from criminal families. On the other hand adolescents rebel; the clergyman's son is a rogue and the workaholic father has a lazy son.

Freud made much of the effects of early training, and the resultant battle between the id and the superego. We have a conscience partly as a result of praise and punishment by our parents and we feel guilty when we go against it even when our desires push us in a different direction. Social pressures unconsciously and consciously mould all of us directly and in-directly through their effect on our parents.

Habit

Doing the right thing comes most easily from having a good character. So we should acquire a good character and good actions will naturally flow from it. The ancient Greeks discussed how we do this. Plato (427-347 B.C.) starts one of his early dialogues by asking Socrates: "can virtue be taught? Or is it not teachable but the result of practice, or is it neither of these, but men possess it by nature or in some other way?"

All three are relevant but Aristotle emphasised habit: "we grow just by the practice of just actions". It helps us to do things we find difficult. The thought of a cold shower appals me. Yet I endured them quite stoically at school. If I took one regularly, the water now would be just as cold but it would be easier to immerse. Habit helps with weakness of the will.

Ask a busy man if you want something done. Ask a person Involved in care if you need care. Sometimes we acquire a caring habit because we like caring, and sometimes because we were obliged to care and just got used to it. The prolonged care that humans have to give children may encourage us to be generally caring.

Certainly those, who lose the habit of doing good things, are less likely to do the good thing, when called upon to make a moral decision. Wrestling professionally with people's problems probably does promote a general concern about other people. It tends to fade with retirement and there is a danger of concentrating on our own happiness. Continuing responsibility, such as the care of grandchildren promotes moral health.

In life we see people with great talents and opportunities, fail in careers and family life, because of character defects, such as laziness, conceit, or lack of common sense. Character is almost everything, and character comes partly from habit.

Tradition

In practice it is easier to get the habit of acting rightly in a society in which it is customary to act rightly. We have good examples to follow. If you do what good people do, you will be good. If you do what happy people do, you have a better chance of being happy. For most of history we have seen goodness in a social setting. We thought it was our duty to practise the virtues admired by our community and the approval of our community fortified us in the practice of those virtues. The community might be our co-religionists, our fellow citizens or our social group.

The mobility of modern life has weakened the force of tradition and the binding power of group loyalty. It has focussed morality on specific problems faced by specific individuals. Some think that the decline of a communal ethic has caused a general decline in standards of behaviour. There are objections to the modern emphasis on solving the problems of the individual and neglecting basic moral tradition. Tradition is a natural guide to good action.

However, there is little evidence that we are less pleasant to each other than we were. Also all societies are imperfect and some more so than others. Reliance on communal values can degenerate to moral relativism, which has serious defects. When natural benevolence or reason tells us that the others in our society are wrong, we must listen to our hearts or consult our brains.

Good examples

It is easier to ask what a good person would do in a situation, rather than work it all out for ourselves. Someone, who generally does good things, is likely to do the right thing in any specific situation. We should model ourselves on good people.

How do we know that someone sets an example, which we should follow? "By their fruit ye shall know them", [Luke 7:44] in other words by their deeds. But then how do we know that their deeds are good? We have to judge that for ourselves. If we approve of most of what they do, then we should probably follow their lead in the particular situation. If people we respect disagree with each other, we must decide for ourselves.

Reciprocity

It is an important mediator of goodness but sometimes it springs from sagacious self-interest. It is probably innate and also predates humanity. If we all return favours, we will receive more favours and we will all be better off. If we all cheat and do not return favours, we will all be worse off. But someone who craftily avoids returning favours in a community, the free rider, will be the best off. At least he will be until they rumble him. So the individual who does not return favours, will prosper and spread his genes in the community. Two genetic tendencies are therefore in opposition. Cheaters will prosper individually, but communities of cheaters will not. The result is likely to be that most communities consist largely of individuals, who reciprocate, but among them will be a minority who do not. That is what we see in practice. Most of us are fairly decent and recognise obligations, but some do not. Experiments show that the best policy in a test situation is to start by playing fair, but to become hostile if your partner does not follow suit.

There are five types of reciprocity; all are socially important and contribute to happiness.

Commercial reciprocity is simple trading, as when a female chimpanzee offers sex in return for delicious fruit, which a male has raided from an orchard at risk. It ties us together by mutual advantage.

Grateful reciprocity is the return of kindness for kindness but with no further expectation. Most of us find it disturbing when we cannot do that.

A former boss worked hard to help me make a vital career step. Many years later he asked me to help his son get a job, and to my chagrin I was unable to do so. Could I have tried harder?

Anticipatory reciprocity is doing a good turn in the hope that the favour will be returned. When the shopkeeper offers you a nice free sample he does it in the hope of your future custom.

Reciprocity is transferred when the favour is done for or returned to one of the benefactor's group, not the benefactor himself. The father is dead so I help the son.

Finally there is altruistic reciprocity. It is the help you give to one in the hope that he will do the same, not for you but for an unknown other or maybe even for no one at all.

A Hindu explained to his son why he gave a little to every beggar (every beggar in India?). As a young man he had been stranded penniless in a distant city, and in desperation asked a Sikh for help. The Sikh gave him the necessary money, but refused to give his name and address for repayment. He told the young man to re-pay him by never refusing a request for help.

Why do we do wrong?

Why do we not do what we know that we should and do what we know we should not? Why do we make others unhappy? Reason, sympathy or both tell us what to do but we fail to do it. As Saint Paul said: "the good that I would, I do not: but the evil which I would not, that I do." [5]

Socrates and Plato thought that evil was essentially igno-rance. When people acted wrongly, they did not know what the right thing to do was. We all act harmfully with the best of intentions out of ignorance. Just think of the awful treatments inflicted by well-meaning doctors on their unfortunate patients in past centuries.

Ignorance can be culpable. It is wilful and culpable ig-norance to campaign against the use of a valuable vaccine. Those campaigners are often suspicious people seeing absurd conspiracies all round them. They think that doctors and gov-ernments are conspiring to expose children to serious risk to save relatively small amounts of money

We deceive ourselves by minimising the harm we do. We have a great capacity to fool ourselves when it suits us. They do not feel pain like we do. They are happier in their hovels. Education would only make them discontented.

Ignorance can be cultural making the individual less blameworthy. Colonists thought that they brought lesser breeds the benefits of religion and civilisation, together with measles, smallpox, alcohol and guns. If we were so often guilty of cultural ignorance yesterday, what makes us think we are free from it today? Aboriginal and mixed race chil-dren in Australia were forcibly taken from their mothers until recently so that they could have the benefits of a European education in an orphanage. In the last century women were sterilised against their wishes, because of incorrect beliefs about heredity.

The Roman poet Ovid (43BC-17AD) knew that even cul-pable ignorance was not a satisfactory explanation of moral failure when he said: "I see the better way, and approve it; I follow the worse." [6] Why do we knowingly act wrongly when we know what we should do and even feel bad about not doing it?

We are good at victimless crimes against faceless people. When we steal from a person, we know that he suffers. But no single person suffers very much, when we steal from the supermarket. The shoplifter persuades himself that it is unimportant if everyone suffers just a little. It is one thing to drop a bomb from an aeroplane flying a mile high; it is another to stick a bayonet in someone's belly. Soldiers deliberately fire wide of the enemy and have to be trained with lifelike targets to shoot to kill. Our species evolved to live in small groups and it is unsurprising that our morality centres on those with whom we have contact.

We can dissociate ourselves from our conscience by just accepting authority and obeying orders. Authority may reside in the priest, the commissar or the man in the white coat. If he says do it, then it must be right. Anyway it is his responsibility.

There are many ways of justifying wrongdoing. We persuade ourselves that we are remedying an injustice done to us. We are not paid as much as we deserve so we are entitled to evade paying income tax. We also use the real or imagined sins of other people as an excuse for our own. Other people are stealing from the office so why should I be different? We can even see ourselves as avenging angels. That horrible rich man deserves to be robbed.

Sometimes we do the wrong thing, because we just do not care that much. We find the cost of doing the right thing greater than we wish to pay. I am in a hurry so I am not going to stop to help a motorist whose car has broken down.

But we also yield to temptation, when we know that we will regret it later. We still make the sarcastic remark, even though we know that the pain from our subsequent guilt will exceed the immediate pleasure at our cleverness.

> I was at a conference, which involved discussing the work of other colleagues. One participant kept talking of distinguished colleagues as his former students in a patronising way. Then he mentioned Sigmund Freud. With difficulty I stopped myself mocking him by saying: "Another of your students?"

The addict knows that he is damaging himself but he cannot stop it. The need for the drug overpowers his fear of the damage that it does to him. We do the wrong thing, knowing that we will be less happy than we would have been, if we had controlled our desire. These failures of the will have some similarity to addiction. What is their explanation? I suppose that rewards and penalties are enhanced by immediacy and diluted by delay. Otherwise believers would never sin. But why do some have the strength to resist when others do not? I can only put it down to an innate quality within the person. We all have different amounts of goodness, innate happiness and willpower. Still as long as doing wrong makes us unhappy we are not lost.

Habit is also as important with doing wrong as with doing right. The secret policeman finds the first cruelty difficult but after that it is just a job. And we also continue with our old faults and our old mistakes, just in new situations or with new excuses. Finally there is that devil in us, which enjoys the unhappiness of others.

8

Our Happiness
Or Their Happiness?

There is no happiness in living just for yourself but no duty to live just for others. We all want to lead happy lives and most of us are happier, if we can make a few other people happy as well. Achieving one goal often helps us to achieve the other. What we most want to take out of this life is our own happiness but it increases our happiness to think that some others are a shade happier because of our existence. At the very least we ought to - and most of us would like to - do overall more good than harm to others, although specific responsibilities may demand rather more than that. Even the birth of most of us brought some happiness to a few people and we would like to think that our deliberate actions also did something for them. But it would be dishonest to claim that we can always reconcile their happiness and ours. There is conflict and we are obliged to balance personal fulfilment against duty.

An attenuating circle of duty extends out from us just as the planets receive less heat from the sun the more distant they are from it. We owe most to our immediate family and after that to extended family, friends and neighbours. Then we have a duty to fellow citizens and all humanity. Finally we owe some care to all creatures, which can feel pleasure and pain.

The analogy to the sun and the planets is imperfect. We may care more for those very near to us than we do for ourselves. The sun sends out its heat impartially but we choose those, whose welfare is dear to us. Special bonds bring closer some who might usually be regarded as more distant. And someone distant to us may have greater need than someone closer to us. But the world would rightly condemn us for choosing a loved pet animal over any human.

Duty to our spouses

In the West a man leaves his parents and cleaves to his spouse, and so presumably does a daughter, although daughters more often keep the aged parent in mind. Young men very easily forget us.

> My daughter's boyfriend went camping in France and telephoned her nearly every day. His mother was reduced to telephoning us to have news of him. It was justice that the young woman ditched him on his return, even though a new interest prompted his dismissal, not disapproval of filial disloyalty.

In the East a woman leaves her parents and joins her husband's family. In the West it is often the daughter, who stays close. Both Western and Eastern ways are right, provided present duties do not cancel past obligations.

A spouse should be an adult, who gave voluntary, informed consent to the most important bargain that many of us will ever make. But consent is not voluntary when a sixteen-year-old girl is bullied by her family into marrying someone she does not know. It is not informed when the prospective bride plans to continue meeting her lover secretly. Parents may know better than their children which partner will make them happy. Arranged marriages may be generally more successful than love matches but without voluntary, informed consent such marriages are wrong in principle and often unhappy in practice.

A woman friend once told me that in marriage women must make the unenviable choice between bores and bastards, because men come into one category or the other. If he is unfaithful with you, he will be unfaithful to you. The good dancer will dance while his wife is in labour. But you can hope that the bore will bore other women.

Although women have the same moral right to choice, independence and career opportunity as men, they may not all be happier for it. The full-time mother may envy the career woman and the career woman may envy the mother. The choice between the two is painful. Trying to do it all is stressful. The best answers come from fairness between spouses.

Swans mate for life but most animals, which live more than a summer, do not. Humans enjoyed or endured monogamy in the Christian West because for most until recently divorce was socially, financially and legally impossible. For good or ill those obstacles to divorce are much less. Now the financially independent woman can leave her boring, balding husband for a more exciting man. I suspect that the new partner becomes equally boring after a few years of the new domesticity. It is a bit like retiring to a place where you enjoyed wonderful holidays. In winter it is as bleak as your home town without the cosy familiarity.

I do not know whether easier divorce has made people happier, although it seems right not to tie spouses together like cats in a bag. People live for so long now that marriages can last sixty years, which is wonderful where there is love and disastrous where there is dislike. If death does not free us these days, then divorce must. Once children are grown and the joint enterprise of raising them is completed, the duty to preserve a marriage reduces. Partners may find that they do not really like each other after the first flush of sexual enthusiasm has abated. The husband, with whom you live, may not be the same man as the one you married and you may not be the same woman.

But there remains a moral duty to give a stable, loving home to the children of a marriage, although the cost of staying with an impossible partner to serve your children's interest may be higher than there is a duty to bear. There is also a residual duty to the spouse, who supported you in your early struggles, however much young flesh excites. Perhaps it would be better, if some alpha males could take an assistant wife instead of abandoning their first one.

The closest marriages can crack under stress. Money worries and children are common causes of stress. Parents often do not agree how to handle the difficult child. Each blames the other for the problems and they find it hard to discuss the problems constructively. Parents should seek professional help but the conviction that it is all the fault of the other partner stops them.

Couples now live together before marriage. There might be even more divorces, if they did not. Before children arrive it is best to know whether or not you still want to live together after easy opportunity has calmed sexual desire and also that you can tolerate lifelong your partner's irritating habits,. The open marriage works for some; partners remain friends living together and have sexual and emotional relationships outside marriage. But often one spouse decides that life would be overall better with the latest love much to the distress of the other one.

Duty to our children

Is there a duty to have children in the first place? There are seven billion of us in our living space, the planet Earth. More than a million extra people appear every week. There are already food and water shortages and each extra human aggravates these and adds to global warming. There are enough of us. Famine, pestilence and war are miserable ways of limiting population. This must mean that as a species we have a duty not to procreate more children than are necessary to replace the present population.

So is it selfish or noble for an affluent couple to remain deliberately childless? We sometimes hear people say that they have made that decision, because it would be wrong to bring children into this dreadful world. But the world is no more dreadful than it always was. Some are just happier pursuing personal interests rather than undertaking the rewarding, exhausting and sometimes disappointing labour of rearing children. It is not selfish to remain childless but doing so misses an opportunity for moral growth and the special happiness in caring for a dependent creature you love like you love yourself.

Rearing well the children we do have is a paramount moral objective. We caused their existence; they did not consent to come into being; they are dependent on us; we gave them an implicit promise to care for them. It follows that we have a duty to sacrifice a chunk of our lives to their welfare, accept damage to our careers and limitations on our pleasures.

Children always need one loving carer in infancy and love and firmness from two parents is better. A nurtured childhood is a happy one and predisposes to success and happiness in adulthood. Children benefit from love from grandparents and affection from an extended family. But as long as they have that one loving carer they can grow up perfectly well without the rest.

They grow up better with a little deprivation. Our natural desire is to pamper them with the electronic toys they crave because their friends have them. Children are even easier prey for the advertisers than adults. But in their interest we should control our natural desire to please them. Television and computer games destroy reading and conversation. Refusal disappoints temporarily but may make them happier in the long run. They must learn that gratifications may be unobtainable, delayed or only obtained at the cost of effort or the forfeit of something else also desired. Money is hard won; friends will always have more than we do. Similarly the child allowed to enjoy junk food will grow up less healthy and less happy.

It is better to know some disappointment as a child, provided childhood is essentially happy. An idyllic childhood is not the best preparation for the griefs and disappointments of adult life. It is better to be a happy adult looking back on an imperfect childhood than an unhappy adult looking back at a perfect childhood. We may blame our failures on our parents but we are usually the authors of our own misfortunes. Short of truly disastrous experiences in childhood we alone are responsible for what we make of our lives. And even when we drew a short straw at birth others have overcome similar problems. We can put only some of the blame onto our childhood. It is an admission of defeat to blame it for too much.

The one thing that every parent is sure to get from children is trouble along the way. If it does not come early, it will certainly come later and perhaps in worse form. You do not know which child will be the comfort of your old age. It will not be the one who is a brilliant success across the ocean. Therefore give your love equally.

You may think that you should decide what is best for your child. With very young children that is what we have to do. But as they grow up they must choose their own path in life, even when they spurn our wise advice. Always be ready with the unwanted advice and just as readily accept its rejection. They know themselves even better than we can know them. They should live with their own mistakes, not those which we imposed on them. They may feel happier blaming us for their failures but we will be happier, if they can't.

Although adults are entitled to their own spirituality, this does not apply to the young in an adult's care. There is a duty to teach them a way of life by instruction and example and present to them a religion, if you have one. How else can they acquire a moral sense? How could you present them with any moral code or religion other than your own? It is what you know best, and presumably you think it is fairly good or you would not be sticking with it. There is a duty to show that you are aware of other value systems. But it is perfectly in order to tell your child that your own code is superior and your own religion has served the family fairly well; it might be easier to stick with the known rather than venture into the unknown. But we have the duty to accept adolescent rebellion and adult freedom of choice.

Duty to our parents

Because of the love our parents gave us and the sacrifices they made for us we owe them a debt of grateful reciprocity. We must consider their happiness but there is no duty to sacrifice our own happiness, if the sacrifice, which their happiness demands, is unreasonable. Good people very close to us can ask too much of us. When our own requirement for happiness is reasonable and theirs is not, we need courage and even ruthlessness to do what is right and grasp happiness.

> A woman once told me that she had refused an of-
> fer of marriage from someone she loved, because her
> parents would have been greatly distressed that her
> suitor's religion was different from their own; they had
> been very good to her. Her parents were long dead.
> She received no further marriage proposals during
> subsequent years. She was lonely and bitterly regret-
> ted her decision. Perhaps her parents would have been
> happier after all to see her happily married.

Duty to our community

We cannot benefit our community in every way so we should do so in ways we enjoy because it means we will do more. The young tend to be idealistic about righting the injustice in the world. In our more mature years some keep the faith and others resign themselves to the unfairness of life and confine themselves to giving practical help to the individuals, who come their way.

Gottfried Leibniz (1646-1715), a German philosopher and mathematician, said:

> …..trying with all our might to contribute to the general good and especially to the embellishment and perfection of that which affects us or that which is near us, that which is so to speak in our grasp. [1]

He believed in moral proximity. You have a duty to your neighbour. Religions tell us to actually love our neighbour, although not his wife, even if she appeals. Actually that is too much to ask and it is quite adequate to be nice to him. It is beyond the call of duty to love him. Who is your neighbour? It is anyone affected by your actions and to a lesser degree by your inactions. But you cannot do everything for everyone, and therefore choice is inevitable. It is right to give preference to those near to us.

Margaret Thatcher, one of the more prominent British prime ministers of the last century, was quite wrong to say that there is no such thing as society. Individual effort and individual philanthropy are important, but so is social cohesion. Alistair Macintyre, a modern philosopher, in his influential book *After Virtue* maintained that the virtues are best exercised as part of a mutually sustaining community. It is certainly easier to act, and especially to sacrifice, in concert with like-minded fellow citizens.

So there are two ways of being a good citizen. One is to help those individuals who come your way and the other is to serve the community in general. Three factors, which accentuate duty, tell us not to neglect what is close at hand. They are moral proximity, the implicit promise made to those near to us to be a good friend to them, and what chance has landed in our laps. William Blake (1757-1827), both artist and poet, said:

> He who would do good to another, must do it in minute particulars. General good is the plea of the scoundrel, hypocrite, and flatterer. [2]

At the end of *Candide*, his novel satirizing the view of Leibniz that this is the best of possible worlds, which God could have created, Voltaire (1694-1778) advised each of us to *cultiver son jardin*. In the *Epic of Gilgamesh*, the oldest moral text known, Gilgamesh after many adventures returns home to rebuild the walls of his own city, Uruk. Unsurprisingly I am selecting quotations and examples, which support the case I am making.

But what can you do as a private citizen beyond being generally helpful to those who cross your path? Let us look at green issues, where we can combine thrift with civic virtue. My pet hate is the four-wheel drive vehicles, with which ladies deliver their children to school but never drive off the road, which is their supposed purpose. When possible leave the car, catch the bus and flash your pensioner's pass. The little green things are rather easy to do. You can switch off the television, not leave it on standby. You can put silver paper behind the radiators. The walls feel much cooler, when you do.

Becoming a blood donor is a superb way of lying down for ten minutes during the working day, and knowing that you are giving direct benefit to a specific, if unknown, person. Do not fear the little needle prick in your arm, because only strong young men swoon. If you are a woman with small veins, warm your hands thoroughly under the hot tap before proffering your arm to the needle.

When you attend hospital there is a duty to allow medical students to practise their examining skills on you. How do you think that the experienced doctor looking after you began to acquire her experience? Is it honourable to benefit from the sacrifice made by past patients for your benefit, and refuse the small sacrifice necessary to benefit future patients? There is also a duty to participate in medical research. Your treatment was improved by the participation of previous patients and it is cheating to refuse to pass on the benefit. When you give informed consent to take part in a study, you are undertaking a joint altruistic project with the doctor. At least you are altruistic, although the doctor may be keen to further her career while she furthers clinical science. If you would accept an organ transplant, then you have a duty to signal your willingness to be an organ donor. We should act as we would wish everyone to act.

The other type of service to others is organised voluntary work, which is a form of service especially suited to the retired. There is a responsibility to make communal institutions work, and so there is a duty to undertake voluntary jobs, which involve time and effort and expose the volunteer to criticism. And one thing is certain; anyone, who makes decisions on behalf of others, even when she has devoted time, thought, effort and money to them, will be criticised whatever decisions she makes. Most criticism comes from those, who could not or would not do the job. But if you are good at it, you should do it, because ability accentuates duty.

On the other hand the wrong people often seek these jobs. If you advertise for an executioner, (perish the thought), unsavoury characters will apply, not those, who would do it expeditiously and with distaste. Plato saw this long ago:

>.....a city in which the prospective rulers are least keen to rule must of necessity be governed best.... and surely it is those, who are no lovers of governing, who must govern. [3]

However, we have to be selective about what Plato says. He also considered that philosophers should be in charge of government (perish the thought twice over). And he never showed any political skills himself. But as we are always governed by those keen to govern he does explain why "with how little wisdom the world is governed." [4]

Although Kant led an uneventful life it is not as safe to be a philosopher as one might think. Socrates was obliged to drink poison. Aristotle fled Athens to avoid suffering the same fate. Boethius (480-525), the last great philosopher of the classical world, was tortured and executed. Machiavelli (1467-1527) was tortured. Spinoza was attacked in the street. Descartes (1596-1650) caught his death of cold attending on the Queen of Sweden. Hobbes (1588-1679) fled to France in the Civil War, because he was a royalist. Nietzsche (1844-1900) went mad. Even death offers no security. Nietzsche was posthumously and quite unfairly adopted by the Nazis. Jeremy Bentham's preserved head was frequently vandalised by students.

Of course different citizens have different duties. The doctor tends the victim and the policeman chases the mugger. It can also be unclear which duty to pursue, as when a sea captain at war may have to choose between saving the lives of

sailors in the sea and attacking an enemy vessel. And sometimes we try to fulfill a duty which we do not have.

> Many of my female patients spoke only Urdu. I tried
> to learn it but settled for Hello and Thank You to show
> friendliness. There is a problem with learning a few
> questions in a language properly, such as a request for
> directions. The answer comes back accurate, fast and
> incomprehensible.

Immigrants should always learn the language of the country
where they have cast their lot. They are at a considerable disadvantage when they do not. It seems right to provide them
with interpreters and translations but that could help to per-
petuate their disadvantage. It might be a better service to put
an emphasis on compulsory, free lessons in the local language
and culture.

9

Reasons To Care About The Happiness Of Others

If seeing the happiness of other people does not bring you happiness, you have three choices.

- Make them happy because God wants you to and your happiness lies in fulfilling God's will.
- Increase the happiness of others as a duty because your happiness lies in doing your duty.
- Have no care for the happiness of others.

Let us suppose that you wish to do God's will. In that case you are making three assumptions.

- God actually exists; he created us and we did not invent him.
- You know what his wishes are. Different religions give different instructions.
- You should obey his wishes. A problem here is that religions can give us instructions, which do not seem to make us or anyone else happy. Rules about homosexuality, abortion, euthanasia and remarriage are examples.

DOES GOD EXIST?

The short answer to that question is that no one can know for sure and actually it does not matter. God surely cares about what you do, not what you think. So believe in what makes you happy. However, it is rather self-centred to hope that belief will secure posthumous bliss for you. You should hope instead that belief will help you to care more for others. And atheists should leave the faith of others alone. There is no reason why people have to be atheists to be happy or to be good to others. Indeed such evidence as there is suggests that believers are probably happier and do more good than atheists. On the other hand religious fundamentalists do more harm than most atheists.

We tend to visualise God as a muscular, middle-aged, European gentleman with a big white beard, as depicted by Michelangelo. We all know that is nonsense. But I have to refer to him as male, because English lacks suitable gender-neutral pronouns. "It" sounds strange, and "she" seems to make God a woman. The apparent sexism is linguistic and cultural, not personal. The traditional joke of European men, who have had a near death experience, is that they saw God and she was black.

I start my concise version of the long answer to the question of God's existence by looking at the arguments in favour of it.

The first cause

Something cannot come from nothing. Every effect has a cause, so there must have been a very first cause of everything and this can only be the entity we call God.

The obvious rejoinder is to ask what caused God. There is always some basic, brute, fundamental, foundational or first fact, from which you have to start. In cosmological terms that might be God, the big bang or whatever came before it. In moral terms it might be the duty to make others happy.

Why are the laws of nature what they are?

If the laws of physics had been slightly different, the universe could not have existed. If the strong nuclear force had been just a little stronger, protons would stick together, and so no hydrogen, no water, and no us. So why are the physical constants exactly what they are?

The anthropic principle is that we are only here to wonder about it because it is like that. But it does not explain why it is like that. A huge coincidence is hardly plausible but there might be some reason, unknown to us, why the physical laws have to be what they are. Another possibility is that there are an infinite number of universes, a multiverse, with universes coming and going like bubbles from a bubble machine. They all have different natural laws and we exist in the one, in which it is possible for us to exist.

Another answer is that one God created one universe suitable for us and maybe for others on other planets. That is the simplest and most comprehensive theory so why should we not all be happy with it in the absence of evidence one way or the other?

But it only suggests that God created the universe about 13 billion years ago and does not show that he intervenes in it. If he does not, then his existence is unimportant. But a non-interventionist god would be a very peculiar thing. It would be like building a complex model railway and then not running trains on it. So is there any evidence that God does intervene in the world?

Direct intervention

There are two proofs that this happens. When God answers prayers he acts through the laws of nature. When he performs miracles he suspends the natural laws.

This argument is weak for two reasons. There is no real proof of such intervention, no proof acceptable to those not committed to believe anyway. For example many miracles are claimed but Hume pointed out that it was far more likely that the witnesses to them were mistaken than that the strange events actually occurred.

No testimony is sufficient to establish a miracle, unless the testimony be of such a kind, that its falsehood would be more miraculous, than the fact, which it endeavours to establish. [1]

Second, the claimed interventions show God as so arbitrary. Why answer some prayers and not other more urgent and important prayers?

> Good men are cruelly disabled by major strokes. At a wake I sat next to a near relative of the deceased. He had treated her with callous, mercenary indifference, letting her die in poverty and distress. He told me that God had answered his prayers and enabled him to survive a series of mini-strokes unimpaired. Why did God spare that dreadful man and not much better men?

Why does God not perform more useful miracles?

> In 1917 Mary, the mother of Jesus appeared three times to three little girls at Fatima in Portugal. A crowd of fifty thousand gathered to witness a re-appearance and saw the sun perform acrobatics.

What could be more irrelevant than this miracle at a time when young men, who had no quarrel with each other, were murdering each other by the hundred thousand in Flanders? It would have been more useful to appear to them and send them home to their anxious wives and mothers.

However, perhaps there is a reason why God does not intervene in any obvious way. Bertrand Russell (1872-1970), an atheist philosopher, was asked what he would say to God, if he met him after his death. He replied that he would ask God why he had provided so little evidence of his existence. God could answer that it would be a mistake to give any positive proofs. We still would not know what he wanted us to do. It would also reduce the virtue in creating happiness, if we acted only out of fear of him.

For the same reason God can't reward the righteous. If we knew that material or social reward regularly followed our good actions, how could we ever be altruistic? However, we are in no danger of that problem. Baruch Spinoza (1632-77) spoke from the heart when he said:

> Daily experience... showed by any number of examples that blessings and disasters befall the godly and the ungodly alike without discrimination. [2]

The origin of species

I will not waste your time refuting creationist arguments. There is ample evidence that the marvellous and diverse forms of life, which inhabit our world, have evolved through natural selection over many millions of years. There is equally no reason why God should not have chosen natural selection as his *modus operandi*.

Personal proofs

These satisfy the believer but she cannot expect them to satisfy anyone else. Philosophy and science have nothing to say and all discussion ends. The agnostic can only answer as Maria, played by the beautiful Natalie Wood, sang in the film *West Side Story* "it's true for you but not for me". [3] The only mistake both believer and unbeliever make is to try to convince each other.

Evil - the argument against God's existence

There is only one argument against the existence of a God we could respect, but it is quite strong. There are two sorts of misery in this world. One comes from natural disasters. Those are best not called evils, as nature has no malign intentions, not being a rational agent. The other sort is the evil which we deliberately do to each other. How can God allow so much of both, if he is omniscient, good and powerful?

> Is the deity willing to prevent evil, but not able? Then he is impotent. Is he able, but not willing? Then he is malevolent. Is he both able and willing? Whence then is evil? [4]

Several answers have been offered. Evil is just the absence of good. Tell that to someone, whose child has just been murdered. There is no evil from God's perspective. Then God must be blind. The worst disasters cannot take away our virtue, which is all that really matters. That is the Stoic answer, often advocated but never practised. Good can come from evil. But why do we need the evil in the first place? We must just accept the will of God. Why should we, when he acts in a cruel and irrational way? Evil is beyond human understanding. Why is evil alone singled out to be beyond our understanding?

How do religions deal with the problem? Islam and Judaism are rather masculine monotheisms, which exhort us to submit to the will of God without question. Christianity offers a God, both human and divine, who suffered with us. The veneration of Mary also gives religion a feminine aspect. It is a powerful story for those with faith. It does not help those, who want evidence, which religion does not offer.

God does not need omniscience to see what misery there is in this world. So can a deficiency in his power or his goodness explain evil? Leibniz thought that this was the best world, which God could have made. His power is certainly limited.

- He cannot create contradictions. He cannot make $1+1 = 3$.
- He cannot change the past.
- He cannot change the future, because he cannot change his mind, as he knows what his mind is going to be.
- He cannot change his nature. "I never give thanks to God for loving me, because he cannot help it." [5]
- He cannot let us experience the wonders of the world without exposing us to its dangers. He cannot give us free will and stop us doing evil.

It is hard to imagine a world, in which a tree can fall in a field, but never on a person. So there have to be natural disasters but do there have to be such terrible natural disasters? A tsunami drowns thousands of people but God was surely clever enough to design a world in which it would not have happened. Why does God allow nature to cause us such unhappiness?

Surely he could also have limited the evil that we do to each other. He could have arranged for Hitler's mother to miscarry and given Stalin his stroke twenty years earlier without limiting our freewill. We would have been spared so much unhappiness. His impotence is not the answer.

If God permits so much unhappiness, can he be good? The Old Testament depicts a God with a tendency to genocide. He kills innocent Egyptian children to achieve a purpose easily obtained by milder means? [6] If he is not good, we should take no interest in him, whether he exists or not.

Conclusion

Arguments about the existence of God are not scientific because there is no proof either way and there is never likely to be. Neither are they of practical importance. God surely cares more about what you do for others than what you think about him. Would you do anything different for others, if you really knew the answer? So the question is of interest only to philosophers. Believe in what makes you happy, especially if it helps you to make other people happier.

How Can We Know God's Wishes?
Why Obey Them?

When we think we are speaking with God, the same areas of the brain light up as when we talk to ourselves. [7] This suggests that it must be very easy to delude ourselves into interpreting our own wishes as those of God. If we look to religion for instruction, we find that the instruction varies with the religion. Most believers follow in their parents' footsteps so the way we interpret God's wishes is dictated by nothing more than accident of birth.

To many Plato is the supreme philosopher. In his dialogue, *The Euthyphro*, he asks this question: are the commandments of God good, simply because they are his commandments, or has God given them to us, because they are good? For which reason should we obey them?

Look at the first option. If everything that God commands is good, would it have been good if he had told us the opposite? The Abrahamic faiths think that God ordered Abraham to murder his son, which is a strange way of showing his goodness. We should not praise Abraham for his blind obedience but rather condemn him for agreeing to do such a wicked thing. The bible is allegorical and interpretation can draw moral lessons from strange stories. But this appalling story seems to advocate obedience to authority against all reason and natural feeling. We should not act wickedly, whoever orders it.

Look at the second option. God only commands what is good. Genesis I gives some support to it, because it says five times that God saw that his works were good. This implies that he used criteria independent of himself to decide that his works and his commandments were good. What are these criteria? If they do not come from God, from where do they come? Should we not use our reason to discover them? When we find out what they are, should we not follow them whether God wants us to or not?

Immanuel Kant said that morality had to be an end in itself. If it were a means to some other end, then it would be downgraded to just a means to that end. We might abandon morality to achieve our real goal. History gives us many examples of the danger of giving priority to a particular view of service to God over what reason and compassion tell us will make for happiness. That brings us back to the nature of morality, wherever it comes from. To me it must fundamentally be about feeling happy and making others happy. Belief in

God is an excellent reason to feel happy and to make others happy.

Why Care About Others, If There Is No God?

Why should you make others happy, if their happiness does not add to yours, if you don't believe in God and you have no sense of duty? Aristotle said: "doing fine and excellent actions is worthy of choice for itself." [8] But you may not find them worthy of choice. Hume summarised the irrationality of helping others at our own cost with his pithy remark: "Tis not contrary to reason to prefer the destruction of the whole world to the scratching of my little finger."

Although that cannot be literally true, the underlying meaning is obvious. It is rational to refuse to put oneself out in the least to help other people for no return. Usually emotion makes us want to do good, and reason helps us decide how to do it. However, you can show me a serious wrong, which I could easily put right, but you cannot make me want to right it. How does one inject empathy, sympathy or a sense of duty into someone, who has no such feelings? If you do not have them, why should you bother? Why should I make you happy, if doing so does not make me happy?

Reasons To Care

I can point out that life is empty for those who have no one to care about.

A youth was questioning a lonely old man: "What is life's heaviest burden?" he asked. The old fellow answered sadly: "To have nothing to carry."

But if total egoism makes me happy, why should I care about your happiness? Why should the uncaring person make himself care and how could he do it, even if he wanted to? Perhaps it is easier to stop yourself caring.

Jack (Legs) Diamond, the American gangster, cared only for his disabled brother. In a film of his life he decided to stop caring about him, so that the other gangsters would not have a hold on him and he let them shoot him.

Would the most selfish person want his children to grow up into the world which his selfishness was creating? But he might not have children or he might want them to be as cynical as himself. A caring society is a happier society. But if everyone cares for me, and I care for no one, I will be happier than all the others. The free rider keeps the penny and eats the bun. My children, born from and nurtured by me, will also be better off than the others. It may catch up with my remote descendants, but why would I care about people I will never see?

We are, as far as we know, the creatures with the greatest capacity to care. We have advanced rationality, morality and spirituality. Julian Huxley, the biologist, wrote in 1930, with remarkable prescience now that our planet home is heating up: "Man… whether he likes it or not, is responsible for the whole further evolution of the planet." [9]

If there is no God and only each one of us to bring happiness into the world, it increases the duty to do it. But that is hardly an argument, if you feel no duty in the first place. The question is unanswered. Why should anyone care?

A reason is not necessary

Does there have to be a reason to care? Everything must start from a first fact or proposition. We have to accept it as fundamental, both uncaused and unexplained. There are first facts in the natural world. The big bang is a cosmological fundamental. Even if one day we do go further back, we will still be left with another unexplained starter fact. What is the fundamental proposition in the moral world, which causes us to care about others? it could be God's wishes, an emotional need or a sense of duty.

But what if they mean nothing to someone? How can I persuade the person without belief, compassion or a sense of duty that he should care? It is best to regard him as suffering from a moral disability, just as others suffer from physical and mental disabilities. Huxley called such people moral imbeciles, comparing them to the tone deaf or the colour blind. [10] The disability may be congenital or result from a failure of care in infancy. The prefrontal area of the brain above the eyes is involved in social and moral behaviour. It is smaller in female adolescents, who show less caring behaviour than normal. Witnessing distress causes electrical activity in that area and an emotional response in normal people but not in psychopaths, who lack empathy and sympathy.

What follows from this? The rest of us have a duty to ensure that one person's disability does not harm others. That applies when the disability is physical, for example infectious disease; mental, for example paranoid schizophrenia; or moral, which we might call psychopathy. We also have a duty to try to prevent or improve any disability, whether it is mental, physical or moral, because disability harms the sufferer. An inability to care leads to social isolation. It deprives the sufferer of a wealth of positive emotion.

Treatment has the best chance of success in children because their brains are still plastic and they mature morally as well as physically and mentally. Our physical and intellectual strength increase with growth, instruction and practice and so can our moral strength. Love and nurture can reduce the expression of bad genes. Also we may treat children according to their long-term interest, when they are too young to give competent consent. Children can be changed.

An American professor of psychology studied psychopathic behaviour. There were several murderers in his ancestry. His genetic makeup was strongly associated with aggression and he had the lack of activity in the prefrontal lobes associated with psychopathy. But he was successful in his professional and family life, rather cold emotionally but in no way psychopathic. He attributed it having been a much wanted and much loved child.

It is difficult to treat adults. The brain is less plastic. Treatment requires consent but that can be encouraged by making it advantageous to accept treatment, knowing that the sufferer will benefit as well as the rest of us. If we insist on good behaviour or if the psychopath decides to behave differently, the new behaviour can become a habit. Adults can change themselves.

A man known for his a furious temper struck his son-in-law. The latter persuaded him to visit his rabbi. He went feeling furious contempt but emerged from a long interview thinking about his life. Next day the milkman put him to the test by spilling milk on the carpet. His eyes blazed fury; he snarled and clenched his fists. But he spoke gentle words. Eventually gentleness became a habit.

It follows that it is just as important to spend money on offenders, whose moral health might be improved, as on the physically or mentally ill. Perhaps Samuel Butler, the Victorian novelist, had a point in his satire *Erewhon* about a country, where illness was a disgrace and crime a misfortune. It follows even more surely that wise investment in the physical, mental and moral health of children is a duty. But social ills are beyond my scope.

10

Should We Really Care About The Happiness Of Others?

Some say that no one has a duty to care about the happiness of anyone else. Some think that others should be caring but they are exempt from that duty. It is more common to think that we should care only about the happiness of some people and pay no heed to the unhappiness of others. There are also those, who do believe that we ought to care about the happiness of others but that there is no possible way of agreeing how to go about it.

I will try to describe these attitudes and their flaws. We all have a duty to care about all others and we all ought to care in much the same way. I cannot prove that we should but such an attitude seems to be universal. Care about the happiness of others is found in all cultures at all times.

Determinism and freewill

In nature events have a cause. Actions are events and we are part of nature so all our actions are caused. They are not voluntary; we could not have done otherwise; we are automata. Free choice is a delusion; everything is predetermined. We may benefit others, because we think we should, but something outside our will makes us think so. Therefore it is illogical to hold ourselves or anyone else responsible for anything we do. Blame, praise and guilt are all nonsense. Whether or not we will try to be happy or make others happy is predetermined like everything else.

This fits with a materialist view of the world. The mind is a function of the brain. Thought is an electrical current circulating between billions of nerve cells. There is no "ghost in the machine". Modern studies have shown that we are not even conscious of most of the thinking that these currents produce. This will not be news to anyone who has gone to sleep with a problem and woken up with the solution. Moreover studies show that the nerve cells, which move a limb, activate before we are conscious of having decided to move it.

There is certainly truth in determinism and recognising it might improve the way in which we run society. Genetic inheritance and early experience predispose us to act in the way that we do. They may make it harder for us to avoid a specific evil. Thus you and I can take alcohol or leave it, although I prefer to take it. But he is different and something in his brain has made him an addict. Lucky Fred has no sexual interest in children but Tom must fight constantly against an inclination, with which he fervently wishes he was not cursed. And Tom claims that sexual abuse in his own childhood has made him what he is. For that he was not responsible.

Even if freewill exists, it has boundaries, which are different for each of us. For example a high percentage of the prison population consists of illiterate adults, those brought up in care homes and people with mental illness. No one chooses to suffer from such misfortunes. So circumstances beyond a criminal's control may have contributed to his criminal tendencies. He is more unfortunate than wicked. Treatment may be more appropriate than punishment. But our sympathy with the misfortunes of others evaporates when those misfortunes inconvenience us.

On the other hand determinism has its limits. Everything we do today was surely not already decided when time began. We certainly have a need to feel that we make choices and inside us we are convinced that we do. A decision made unconsciously might still be voluntary. And even if we do not have freewill, we still have free won't. When our decisions rise to the conscious level, we can interpret, adjust or reject them.

But the real answer to determinism is a resounding "so what!" Would you do anything differently, if you knew it were absolutely true? Even in a determinist world harm and benefit remain and we can still regard the one as a good and the other as an evil. Nothing stops us preventing evil and promoting good.

No society could exist without a concept of personal responsibility, bringing rewards and penalties for actions. Even if a man cannot help having paedophile desires, we have to act as though it is his duty to control them, because of the harm he does by giving way to them. People can and do control such desires, either because they know they are wrong or because they fear punishment. If we hold other people responsible for their actions, it follows that we should hold ourselves similarly responsible.

What does it matter why we feel happy about helping and bad about harming others? The world is a happier place for all of us, if we act morally and teach our children to do the same. Determinism does not stop us praising, blaming, rewarding and punishing others or feeling responsible ourselves. However, it is not just an abstract philosophical concept. It reinforces moral modesty. We should be cautious with judgement, because we may not realise what there has been in someone's past, which made them act in that way.

Egoism

Choice is voluntary and we can talk about it rationally but it is always selfish. We make others happy just to feel happy ourselves. Care about the happiness of others just boils down to care about our own happiness. Thomas Hobbes, the father of English political philosophy, made that claim.

> ...and of the voluntary acts of every man, the object is some good to himself...in hope to gain the reputation of charity, or magnanimity; or to deliver his mind from the pain of compassion; or in hope of reward in heaven. [1]

So the first question to answer is whether all that I do to promote your happiness I do purely to further my own. That is often but not always true. The man who rushes into a burning house to save a child, has no time to fear guilt, if he does not act. He just does it because he is that sort of person. What about those who resist torture in order not to betray their comrades? Their heroism springs from conviction, loyalty, courage and determination. Fear of guilt feelings is not upper-most in their minds. On a more mundane level the man toiling up a mountain to scatter his friend's ashes may simply have taken a decision to keep a promise.

But actually Hobbes is saying what Hume said later. We help others because it makes us happy and it makes us un-happy when we don't. If you do not have such feelings, you are not a good person. Aristotle said: "No one is good if he does not enjoy fine actions". [2] Virtue lies in being the sort of person who is made happy by the happiness of others, and distressed by their distress.

Good actions are associated with good people but we are all patchwork quilts of good and bad. People act out of normal character and then we must recognise the good action of the mainly bad man and *vice versa*.

Aristotle taught the virtue of the mean. He advocated gener-osity not extravagance or miserliness. But moderation did not rub off on his famous pupil, Alexander the Great. He applied to succeed Plato as head of his Academy and left Athens in high dudgeon when a well-connected mediocrity was appointed. Many of us have felt that way but with less justification. Later he opened the Lyceum in Athens (for philosophy, not dancing or bingo). He again left Athens in a hurry for fear that the citi-zens would encourage him to follow in the footsteps of Socrates. The Athenians took philosophers more seriously than we do and they disliked Macedonians like Aristotle. He was a kindly man, who freed his slaves and asked his executor to find his widow someone nice, if she wanted to remarry.

Excluding yourself from duty

Frederick Nietzsche challenged the caring ethic. He rejected a universal morality: "the requirement of one morality for all is really a detriment to higher men." [3] He regarded Christian morality as a device of the weak to frustrate the natural superiority of the strong. He championed:

> the healthiest and most primal human instinct: the will to power, the lonely quest for mastery of life's difficulties, the indefatigable striving that disdains the deadening narcotics of traditional morality and mass conformism.

His is an ethic of self-fulfilment. It is following your star to the exclusion of the interests of others, especially those of the weak. There is a grain of truth in Nietzsche's philosophy because sometimes we should follow our star. But it only works, if others accept your privileged status. Why should they? They will reasonably either claim an equal right to the privilege or deny it to you. What gives me the right to decide that I will not be bound by the rules, which others accept, especially as it suits me that they should accept them?

Narrowing the focus

Most of us think that all rational beings should have some concern for all sentient beings, especially humans. Some exclude specific human groups from that duty, negating its universality. It is usually prejudice of Type 1 or Type 3 [p 86].

There is racial exclusion. For example Hutu extremists were dehumanising Tutsis by calling them cockroaches before the genocide in Rwanda. There is social exclusion. "God made us high or lowly and ordered our estate", says the hymn. That was the religious confidence trick the rich worked on the poor. The rich never asked themselves whether their estate was originally acquired by means, of which God would have approved. There is national exclusion. Nationalism in its benign form is a manifestation of moral proximity – we all pull together. In its extreme form it becomes moral exclusivity. It devalues a smaller or greater part of humanity and absolves us from applying the caring ethic to them. Sadly hostility to other groups helps cohesion within the group.

Political morality

Niccolo Machiavelli was the great exponent of this. The claim is that those, whose duty it is to further the happiness of many, are allowed to cut moral corners in order to do so. They may protect our wellbeing by means which we would not accept in private life. The rest of us are often happy to let them do this. We judge politicians and generals by results and we are not too worried about how they obtained them. More hangs on their success than on the good deed of the individual.

Politicians lie to us because unpleasant truths make us unhappy and we shoot the messenger. Actually these days we just do not re-elect the politician. They also lie to us for our own good and we judge them by whether it turns out to be for our good.

Themistocles, the Athenian statesman, was convinced that the Persians would attack Greece again and that Athens should invest in warships for protection. But the Athenians would not believe him. So he persuaded them that the nearby island state of Aegina was a danger, which it was not. And they did invest in the ships, which helped to save them from the Persians.

In contrast, Neville Chamberlain, the British prime minister at the outbreak of the Second World War, was an honest man who believed the word of the German chancellor.

In 1938 Chamberlain agreed in Munich that Hitler should annex a large part of Czechoslovakia. He did so in return for a written promise from Hitler that he would not gobble up any more countries. Hitler was amused to give the nice gentleman his autograph. Chamberlain returned to London in triumph waving his piece of paper to cheering crowds. He declared that he had secured "peace for our time." Chamberlain was slow to make Britain ready for war. It came within a year after further Nazi aggression.

Who served his nation better, Themistocles, the wily Athenian, or Chamberlain, the upright Englishman? Margaret Thatcher said of another politician that niceness is not enough. We want politicians to look after our interests and care much less whether they are virtuous.

We must distinguish between the immoral action done on behalf of others from that done exclusively for oneself. Anyone in a position of power is wrong to accept a bribe. But should we criticise a businessman for obtaining employment for his fellow citizens by paying a bribe in a foreign country to secure a business contract? If bribery is the only way to do business in that country, what else can he do? Public gain is not private gain; the danger is blurring the distinction between personal and general happiness.

Morality Is Personal

I do what I think it is right for me to do. You do what you think you should do. We may do different things in the same situation but neither of us should criticise the other.

Emotivism

Accepting that moral choice is free and may be unselfish, it might still be entirely personal and emotional. Such choices cannot be meaningfully discussed. A Viennese school of philosophers in the last century put forward that claim.

There are only two types of meaningful statement. "Stealing is taking property without permission" is an analytic sentence, which simply defines stealing. "Stealing causes distress" is a synthetic statement of fact, which can be verified empirically. "Stealing is wrong" is just an emotional outburst telling us what we personally feel about stealing and what we think others ought to feel about it. It says nothing about why you or anyone else should feel that way. So it has been called the Boo! Hurrah! school of moral philosophy.

But the emotional response to stealing has a rational basis. We give each other reasons why stealing is wrong. It harms others, and once we accept that harming others is wrong, it is rational to condemn stealing. Happiness is a fact for us and for others, not an opinion. Even when our decisions are emotional, we justify them rationally. A J Ayer (1910-89) was the leading British exponent of this philosophy. However, Ayer must often have debated moral choices with himself and discussed them with others. He chose deliberately; he did not just act impulsively.

Ayer published his bestseller, *Truth, Language, and Logic* when he was 26 years old. Philosophical tracts are rarely bestsellers. The rest of his professional life was an anti-climax. On the other hand, if success comes towards the end of life you have no time to enjoy it. Never expect to win all the way. His experience was different from that of Hume, who said: "Never literary attempt was more unfortunate than my *Treatise of Human Nature*. It fell dead-born from the Press." Authors would always rather be criticised than ignored.

Intuition

A moral intuition is an immediate certainty in the mind about what it is right to do in a situation, without any preliminary reasoning. That applies if I think that the right thing is to make you happy. It also applies, if I think that the right thing is to obey the dictates of some church. Most of our moral decisions are made like that, either because there is no time or because we feel there is no need for rational thought in the circumstances. We could hardly live otherwise. In real life we do not consider our principles and then decide what to do in a situation. We act and we explain our action when necessary by an appeal to principles.

Neuroscience has shown that these snap decisions are accompanied by electrical activity in a primitive brain area. A moral sense resides in the brain below the level of consciousness. But when we think more deeply about moral decisions activity shifts to the frontal cortex, which evolved more recently. This is to be expected. Lower animals also make snap decisions, which they inevitably make in more primitive brain areas, as they do not have a large frontal cortex. Some apes may have a rudimentary moral sense, but only humans can ponder decisions, because only they have the large frontal cortex and the language, with which to do it.

Intuitions are analogous to feelings of disgust, for example innate revulsions against foul tastes and foul smells. We have developed these feelings because foul smelling and foul tasting substances are usually injurious to the health. It is an instrumental disgust, which has become internalised. Intuitions probably arise similarly. Some actions are good and some are bad for the community and we internalise the general attitude to them. So intuitions tend to be common to the group.

Is intuition or moral reasoning the better guide to acting for the best? The question is akin to asking whether it is better to do good out of sympathy or out of duty.

> Himmler, the SS commander, was very concerned that the concentration camp guards might be troubled by compassion, when they had a clear moral duty to continue the patriotic task of murdering their prisoners. [4]

> In Mark Twain's *Huckleberry Finn* Huckleberry hides the runaway slave Jim out of compassion for him. It troubles him that he is doing wrong, because he is lying and defrauding Jim's owner of her property. In that society a slave was property. Even worse, he knew the lady, who owned him.

Huck did well to follow his heart. The moral reasoning which opposed his intuition, was flawed. He owed no respect to a law which treated a man like a chattel. He was also right to use a bad means, lying, to achieve a good end.

But intuitions and feelings can be wrong. I am horrified at the idea of giving my children fried caterpillars to eat. But if there is no other food, I would be wrong to deny them that nutritious and probably savoury meal. Intuition is often not enough. The results of following it may be disastrous; other people have opposing intuitions; we may have no intuition about what to do. Reason is necessary to justify, overcome or replace intuition. The heart should be guided by the head.

Jones steals bread to feed his starving children and intuitively we support him. We justify our intuition by reasoning. The consequence of children starving is graver than an unfair loss to a baker. The duty to obey the law is diminished in a society, which allows children to starve.

Smith steals from his employer in England to give the money to a children's charity. Although we do not condemn Jones, we intuitively condemn Smith. There is a rational basis for doing so. Jones has greater moral proximity to his children than does Smith to children who he does not know, and who are not specifically his responsibility. Smith lives in a more moral society than Jones, which increases the duty to obey the law.

The first moral of these stories is that we need to think about our moral intuitions. The second moral is that Increasing the sum of happiness in the world is not everything. How we go about it is important.

Existentialism

This is another individualistic approach to moral decisions. It loomed large in the last century. Its leading exponent was the French philosopher and novelist, Jean Paul Sartre (1905-80). He famously contrasted a person with a paper knife. The paper knife is made with a purpose in mind. In the jargon its essence precedes its existence. But a person's existence precedes his essence. He makes his own choices in the world into which he is born. He is "condemned to be free". He must think about his decision, not rely on intuition, but the decision is peculiar to the individual. He must do what he is happy with.

The objection to this philosophy is that unless my situation is significantly different from yours we both ought to do the same thing. There has to be a reason why it is right for me but not for you.

Sartre preached to his disciples in a Parisian café. I sat there over a coffee, hoping for enlightenment, which came with the realisation that the coffee was just like everywhere else. Sartre rather over emphasised our moral freedom. The French admire intellectuals more than the English. Sartre could choose from his prettiest students even though he was small, ugly, and had a bad squint. Perhaps that made him think that we could all pick the cherry of our choice.

Relativism

This bases itself on what the group feels to be right. There is no universal moral code. Even if it is absurd for the individual to have his own moral system, irrespective of his society, why should not each society have its own moral system, regardless of other societies? What we happen to think is right in our neck of the woods really is right in our neck of the woods. The same applies to you in your society. Do in Rome as the Romans do. So there is no difference between normative ethics, what we should do, and descriptive ethics, what we actually do. Tradition is the key to general happiness.

It just simply cannot be true. What was right in Hitler's Germany or Stalin's Russia was simply not right. Societies can be grossly perverted or mistaken about some issues. A few hundred years ago in the UK children were hanged for theft. They thought it was right then and now we think they were wrong. We don't just think it would be wrong to hang children now; we think they were wrong to do it then. It was wrong because the punishment is disproportionate; children should not be judged like adults; and a society, which allows children to suffer want, is itself guilty.

> Socrates was executed in Athens for filling the minds of young men with dangerous ideas. However, he could have had sexual relations with his male students with general approval. Today he would have been wiser to stick to unconventional ideas.

Which era had the right attitude? It depends on some difficult to determine facts. How much harm did such sexual relations do then? How much harm do they do now? How much harm did attacking received wisdom do then? How much would it do now? Moral principles do not change but moral judgement depends on situations. To that extent relativism is right. It is also important not to mistake cultural relativism for moral relativism.

> A Levantine king in classical times asked both the Greeks and the Indians how much money they would require to burn, and how much to eat the bodies of their dead parents. The Indians said that they needed

no money to eat Mum and Dad, who would expect to join the funeral feast in that passive capacity. But they rejected with horror the idea of burning them. The Greeks replied in similar vein, the other way round.

Both were honouring their parents and that can be done in whatever way is culturally appropriate. Westerners put the dead in the ground to be eaten by worms. Parsees put them in the open to be eaten by vultures, which gives them a problem now that vultures are scarce in India. Custom varies legitimately with culture but not right and wrong.

Morality Is Universal

The alternative view is that all rational beings should care about the distress and the happiness of all creatures that can experience benefit from their care. Obviously we will care more for those we feel near to and we sometimes have to decide whether to put our own happiness before that of others. But this caring principle seems to emerge everywhere as a fundamental basis for human behaviour. Like the existence of God it is a starting point, which cannot be proved.

Caring predates writing, religion and even humanity. There is evidence that Neanderthals and even earlier hominids cared for wounded brethren. I suspect that aliens in other worlds probably do so also, if they are rational, social creatures. Moral texts, which most of us would approve today, occur quite soon after the invention of writing, and they all preach a caring ethic. Concern for the happiness of others is widespread in societies separated by thousands of years and thousands of miles

A Babylonian Counsel of Wisdom from about three thousand years ago says:

- To the feeble show kindness,
- Do not insult the downtrodden,
- Do charitable deeds; render service all your days.
- Do not utter libel; speak what is of good report,
- Do not say evil things, speak well of people.

The Buddha was a prince in Northern India, with a background in Hinduism. He abandoned a comfortable life for asceticism and contemplation. Like Confucius he lived around the sixth century BC, so it was a good time for moral thinking. Four of his basic precepts are:

- Keep from harming any living thing; practise love.
- Keep from taking what is not given; practise charity.
- Keep from wrong sexual conduct; practise purity.
- Keep from lying; practise sincerity and honesty.

In his Sermon on the Mount Jesus said that when struck on one cheek we should turn the other. This shows an exemplary rather than an obligatory concern for the happiness of those, who might not deserve to be happy. Another view is that evil flourishes if good men are silent. But Jesus was counselling forbearance, when we suffer evil ourselves, not passivity towards evil in general.

One and a half thousand years later and four thousand miles to the west, Manco, the last Inca, addressed his people before leading a revolt against the conquistadors in 1535.

Remember the Incas, my ancestors, ruled from Chile to Quito, treating their vassals so well they might have been their own children. They did not steal and they killed only when it served justice. They kept order and reason in the provinces as you know. The rich were not over proud; the poor were not destitute. [5]

Also in 1535 four Spaniards, Cabeza de Vaca and three companions, came to the end of a long journey westward across Texas and Mexico, in which they befriended and were befriended by the local tribes. They finally met Spaniards approaching from the other direction, intending to enslave the Indians. The Indians refused to believe that de Vaca and his companions shared a common origin with their compatriots. He writes:

The Indians said the Christians lied. For we had come from the sunrise, the others from where the sun set. We cured the sick, the others killed the healthy; we went naked, while the others went in fine clothes on horseback with weapons. And also we asked for nothing and gave away all that we were given, while the others seemed to have no other aim than to steal what they could and never gave anything to anybody. [6]

Fortunately most of us have an innate need to relieve distress and promote happiness but some will always exclude some others from consideration.

11

How Should We Go About Making Others Happy?

If we want to make other people happy, we need to know how to go about it. Moral principles guide us in two ways. They tell us what to do in a situation. They also limit the ways, in which we may try to make people happy. In general they tell us what to do in life.

A principle tells us what our objective should be in a situation. Look! He is drowning. I believe in the principle that we should save life, so my specific objective in this situation is to save his life and my action is to throw him a lifebelt.

Hume pointed out that the situation itself does not tell us what to do. He famously said that "is" does not imply "ought". The "ought" comes from a moral principle. A general moral principle indicates a specific objective in a specific situation and that prompts a specific action. We connect the action in the situation to the general principle by the specific objective, saving his particular life. [1]

> David Hume and his friend Adam Smith (1723-90), the econ-omist, were the two great minds of the Scottish enlighten-ment. Hume was the first philosopher to openly avow atheism and he died firm in that faith. He was intellectually brilliant and physically so clumsy that the French king allowed him to turn his back on the royal presence and leave it walking forwards. During his life he was better known as a historian than a philosopher. If the public ignore you, posterity may adore you or more prob-ably forget you.

Not all principles of conduct are moral. "Always look after number one first" is a principle of conduct, but following it will not make anyone else happy, so here it is not my concern.

Principles are searchlights illuminating situations but applying different principles to the same situation is like shining a red light or a green light into a dark room. You will see different things, and although they are all there, each light shows a different scene, which may suggest a different action. My duty to relieve distress tells me to help him die but my duty to respect life tells me to refuse his request.

Moral principles do not themselves conflict but the objectives derived from them do. We should not lie and we should not hurt people. Sometimes these principles seem to be in conflict but it is the objectives derived from them, which are in conflict. Should I tell this particular lie to avoid this particular harm?

There are no exceptionless moral principles. However binding a principle seems the objective derived from another principle will sometimes be so important that it must take priority in this case. Perhaps you should not agree to worship idols even to save your life. But perhaps you should do so to save the life of your child.

Could there be a moral rule, which brooks no exception? Certainly harming someone, just because we enjoy his suffering, as with the bully, is always wrong. That is irrelevant because the bully is not trying to act morally. Moral principles are guides to acting morally. There is sadly room for self-deception. The boxing fan claims that he only goes to see the skill but he does enjoy the blood.

Two basic principles

We start with a fundamental duty to care about the happiness of others but we need to know what to do in practice. Our initial guidance comes from two very basic principles, the Kantian categorical imperative and the Golden Rule, "do as you would be done by". Kant called his imperative categorical, as opposed to hypothetical, because we must obey it at all times. One version of his imperative affirms the universality of morality.

> Act as if the maxim of your action was to become through your will a universal law of nature. [2]

In simpler words, do as you think others should do. German philosophers are known for the depth of their thinking, not the clarity of their writing. His maxim puts the emphasis on the agent and his duties. Make your actions such as you hope to see from everyone. It tells me that I must not allow myself to do something, because I am Tom, if I think Harry would be wrong to do it. It excuses me from donating to the cats' home, as long as I do not hope that others will.

> I did once donate to a cat's home, taking the note from my wallet without really believing it. The wife of an esteemed friend died. They had no children and loved cats. At the funeral the nominated charity was the cats' home. A refusal to give would have been disrespect to my friend. Not giving the money to a children's charity instead was a failure of care. Objectives derived from different principles clashed.

If we want to live together in justice and harmony, we could not do better than obey Kant's imperative. But it needs interpretation. We are not required to act in the same way, if our situation is not the same. Wives in general should not leave their husbands. It is not good for society that this should happen often. But this particular wife might have overwhelming reasons to leave this particular husband. The more general the rule the more often we will find exceptions.

Different agents have different duties in the same situation. One person cooks for the invalid and another nurses him. We should each fulfil our assigned function. If your brother and mine are drowning, my first duty is to rescue my brother and yours is to rescue yours. The rule becomes that everyone should rescue his own brother first. We should act as we would wish everyone to act, if in the same personal situation and faced with the same circumstances. There must be a lot of room for self-deception.

The imperative needs modification as well as interpretation. We admire saints and heroes but we do not copy them and they do not expect us to. I doubt whether Saint Francis wanted everyone to act like him. If we were all saints and heroes, society would be very strange. Kant's imperative seems to be directed at a human norm but some exceptional people want to exceed the standards which they expect of others.

> In Somerset Maugham's book, *The Moon and Sixpence*, the narrator goes to Paris to bring back Strickland, who has deserted his family to become an artist. The story is loosely based on the life of Gauguin. The narrator quotes Kant to the effect that it would be disastrous, if everyone did what Strickland had done. Strickland replies that very few would want to do what he has done.

Perhaps some exceptional people are not required to live up to the norm in some respects, because doing so would stop their genius benefiting mankind. This harks back to the emphasis on the results politicians get, not the methods they use

Kant allowed no exceptions to his rule. Under no circumstances would he approve of suicide, because you are using yourself as an object, or of lying, because you must not break the moral rules dictated by reason. But we can all imagine circumstances, in which suicide or lying would be right.

Kant's imperative must be supplemented by The Golden Rule, which emphasises the object of action. Treat everyone as you want to be treated yourself. We have duties to others and they have rights. Jesus put it positively: "Do unto others as you would have them do unto you." [3] This requires of us beneficence, tempered by respect for the object's autonomy. As we usually want others to do nice things to us, it is a fairly demanding principle.

It also has a weaker, negative form: "Do not inflict on others what you yourself would not wish done to you" as Confucius put it. [4] This is less demanding, because it requires inaction, rather than positive action.

Implicit in both formulations is a hope that others will treat us as well as we treat them. I treat him like me because he is like me, and he should do the same for me, because I am like him. That is how to further our common happiness.

The Golden Rule also needs interpretation. It helps us to know the right way to treat other people and express care. Just consider how you would like to be treated yourself. That is not an infallible guide, as a friend found when he introduced a closet homosexual to a pretty girl. The hearty extrovert assumes that everyone likes swimming in the cold sea, as he does. It is important to realise that others are not as we are. They know what is good for them and the underlying principle is to treat them as they want to be treated. Nevertheless we do not have to do anything wrong, because someone wants us to. That negates the fundamental caring duty we owe to all. For the same reason we refuse requests from a person to do something, which we think would harm him.

The Golden Rule fails at the extremes, as do all principles. You are a saint and give me all your lunch but you would not expect me to give you all mine. You are a crook and would despise me if I did not cheat you, because you would certainly cheat me. Nevertheless I should not cheat you.

Kant did not like The Golden Rule. He said we should treat others in the way that the moral law, derived by reason, tells us to treat rational beings, not according to their desires. But the purpose of the moral law is to promote the welfare of others. He says you should not lie even to save the life of your friend. Here he is wrong. There are exceptions to every principle. Unfortunately following moral principles rigidly does not always promote happiness.

SPECIFIC PRINCIPLES

Moral principles can be related to the agent, the object or both, to the categorical imperative or to the Golden Rule.

Respect for autonomy

This principle derives from the Golden Rule and centres on the object of action. The caring duty tells us to benefit others but the principle tells us not to impose benefit on them, if they do not want it. We would hate others to impose unwanted benefits on us. We must respect each other's right to decide what is good for each of us because we all usually know best what suits us personally. The doctor is the expert on patients but the patient is the expert on himself. The law in most countries protects the citizen from beneficial coercion. The doctor can only advise the patient to have the operation. I know you should give up smoking but I must not throw your cigarettes away.

There are limitations to this principle. We impose our will on children when they do not understand what is at issue. People with dementia are similarly incompetent with regard to the need for a particular action. The law will sanction the imposition of unwanted benefits on them. The duty of care may cry out to us to overrule the stupid decision of a competent adult. We would be right to restrain a man from rushing into a burning house to save a dog. We would argue that he was temporarily irrational. The physical assault is temporary and relatively minor. When the roof falls in, realisation of the stupidity of his decision and gratitude to us for stopping him acting on it will not be long delayed.

A man with young children refuses surgery for a curable cancer. Without it he will die with misery and guilt for what he has done to his family.

He is in the grip of a phobia, so he is not rational. Or he has an unwarranted faith in natural healing, so he makes his decision on the basis of a false belief about reality. Persuasion, second and third opinions, and the pleas of his family and friends do not move him. So perhaps he is not truly competent. The law puts defence of our liberty before our duty to be sensible. Professional codes and common sense preclude the use of force. What is the moral argument here? If he would never be grateful for what we have done, there is no case for action, because there would never be benefit to him. If we can be reasonably sure that he would be grateful later, there is a moral case for overriding his autonomy. We also have a duty to his family, who are dependent on the preservation of his health. The weakness of that moral argument is that we would be using him solely as a means to benefit others. In fact practicalities and legal issues stop us operating forcibly on an adult. How can we take him struggling to the operating theatre? On the other hand I remember a determined, sensible woman, who bullied her mother into submitting to cancer surgery in the face of a phobia. Morality is always situational.

Honesty

Both the two basic principles support a principle of honesty. We do not want people to lie to us so we should not lie to them. And we do not think other people should lie so nor should we. Life is impossible without a measure of trust in what we are told. How would we safely shop, if the fishmonger said that the fish was fresh, when it was frozen?

The duty to volunteer a truth, which someone needs to know, and the duty not to lie are related but different principles. There is even a duty to tell painful truths, if there is a reasonable expectation that action can be taken, which will avoid greater distress later. If he is drunk tell him so or he may do something, which he will regret.

On the other hand Alfred Adler, the psychoanalyst, said: "the truth is often a terrible weapon of aggression. It is possible to lie, and even to murder with the truth." [5] There are times when we should not tell the truth. You should not tell a dying woman that her son had been killed in a road accident.

The redoubtable Liverpool MP, Bessie Braddock, told Winston Churchill that he was drunk. He wittily replied that she was ugly, but tomorrow he would be sober. Though we laugh with Churchill, he was wrong and she was not. He could sober up but she could do nothing about her face.

Conversely it is wrong to leave people in ignorance of facts important to them. It is culpable inaction. Similarly answering a question with correct facts, knowing that we are not giving the information, which is really needed, is akin to lying. As the intention and effect are to mislead in the same way that a lie does, the moral difference is not great.

Lying to take advantage of another is wrong but even lying with good intention is dangerous.

A man died sitting in his dressing gown by his hospital bed. Two nurses laid him out and then one went for lunch. The other noticed in the register that he was Jewish and telephoned the rabbi for instructions. He told her not to touch the body. So she dressed him and put him back in the chair. The other nurse came back from lunch, looked behind the curtain, screamed and fainted. [6]

A good story has more than one moral. The road to hell is paved with good intentions. More practically, keep your colleagues informed about what you do.

But our life together depends on lies. Graham Greene, the novelist, said: "in human relations kindness and lies are worth a thousand truths." [7] When the secret police knock on your door and ask whether your friend is hiding in your house, you tell them that he has already left on the train. Betrayal is a greater sin than lying. When the dying woman asks after her dead son you lie.

We are also allowed to lie to protect ourselves from unjust harm. We lie to the secret police. At a trivial level people ask personal questions when they do not need to know the answer and we do not wish to give it. Sometimes it is malicious and sometimes mouths open before minds engage. Of course a clever answer is best, but we slow witted people only think of it as we are going down the stairs after the party. Telling someone to mind their own business implies that you have a problem. It is not wrong to lie, if that seems the best course of action. It is not wrong, because no one has any justified benefit from the truth and you are harmed by it.

Then there are the trivial lies we all tell to spare another's feelings, the white lies. They must fulfil certain conditions. They benefit the hearer not the teller, unlike the standard lie. There is a sincere belief that the hearer will be happier both now and later, if we comfort him with a lie instead of distressing him with the truth. We think he would prefer to hear a lie rather than the truth so we are respecting his autonomy. The liar will not be ashamed, if the lie is revealed. We would all suffer if we confronted others with distressing truths, for which there was no remedy.

In some cultures the white lie concept is pushed further than in others. Courtesy demands that you always tell your interlocutor what you think he wishes to hear. Society does not break down because everyone understands the game. When cultures meet, misunderstandings occur. I sometimes found that young colleagues from Asia refused to disagree with me about cases. But I wanted them to, because I needed a vigorous discussion to help me make up my own mind.

There may be a duty to lie to those not competent to decide their best interests, although we always put our future credibility at risk when we do so.

For years my mother combed my thick, curly hair by telling me that she had just caught a nit. I knew that, if a single nit hatched, little boys were taken to the cleansing station where dreadful things were done to them with hosepipes.

We meet people, who say: "are you calling me a liar?" Usually they are liars, because it would never occur to honest people that anyone would think they were lying. Honest men make bad liars; the confidence tricksters sound the most sincere. Verisimilitude trumps veracity in the law courts. We also deceive others best by deceiving ourselves first because then we do not unconsciously give away clues, which others unconsciously pick up.

Women often make better liars than men, not because they are more dishonest but because they have superior social skills. Or perhaps frequently faking orgasms makes them more adept. And a minority have always cleverly obtained the best genes from one man while persuading another man, more suited to rearing their child, to accept it as his own.

Slippery slopes

This is an agent directed principle. If we start doing small wrong things we will finish doing big wrong things. Why should this be? We have weak wills and it is easier to keep a door shut than half open. (In some ways it is easier to give up drugs than to lose weight permanently. You can forswear drugs completely but everyone still has to eat.)

We deceive ourselves very easily. Fiddling the expenses just can't be wrong because everyone else in the office is doing it. We are creatures of habit and after we have done it a few times we do it all the time. And then we start to slide down the slippery slope. We claim a little more mileage than we should, and finish by claiming for journeys which we never took.

Slippery slopes are dangerous even when our intentions are good and then they tie up with the ends and means problem. It may seem right to torture a terrorist to make him reveal where he has hidden his bomb. But if our police start to use torture for one good reason, they will find plenty of other good reasons to use it, and eventually it will become standard practice. It is easy to finish by perpetrating more evil than one prevents. We kill terrorists, even when doing so risks the death of a child. We finish by killing more children than terrorists.

But life is messy and it is hard to do pure good. So what should we do? An Archbishop of York pointed out that it is possible to slide a little way down a slippery slope, without gliding helplessly to the bottom. To avoid that danger it is necessary to look carefully at the slope and decide how much sliding will be permitted, and which steps we will not allow ourselves to take. It is important to erect a fence on the slope, which will stop us slipping too far. For example when police suspect someone of serious crime, aggressive questioning may be right but never to the extent that it might make an innocent man confess.

Means and ends

Achieving a good end through some bad means is always worrying, often dangerous and sometimes mistaken. Some go further and claim that you must never do a wicked thing to achieve something good. Ends cannot justify means. It is an agent directed rule.

But good actions sometimes have unavoidable bad effects, a double effect. It is a good wind that blows no one any ill. In the last world war the allies knew that bombing military targets in Germany would also cause the death of innocent civilians. Everyone agrees that actions with mixed effects can be permissible. Aquinas studied this problem and devised rules. [8]

- The good must outweigh the bad.
- We must not want the bad to happen, even though we know it will.
- There must be no safer way of achieving the good.

We can all agree with those three restrictions but his next two are more problematic.

- The action must not itself be intrinsically wrong.
- The bad must not be the means by which the good is achieved.

As a young man I worked at a hospital, where the nurses were mainly Irish, and devoutly Catholic. They were withholding pain relief from dying patients out of fear that they might accelerate death, and thus commit a terrible sin. The priest was obliged to expound in a sermon the error, which they were making. When the intention is to relieve pain, it is permissible to shorten life as a side effect of the means necessary to relieve the pain.

Mixed effects are often unavoidable but there is good reason to be concerned about using wrong means for good ends. If you do a bad thing, then for whatever reason you do it, bad has been done. There is no chance that the bad will not happen, but the good may never materialise. So if you are going to flout the principle, it is necessary to be as sure as possible that the good will actually happen. It is better if it is not too long delayed. Those, who worked for the communist revolution, justified cruelty, dishonesty, and treachery by their utopian goal but their goal was a mirage. Also those you want to benefit must accept your goal as a benefit. There is no right to despatch people unwillingly to your version of heaven.

There are also problems about accustoming ourselves to doing bad things even with good motives. It is a slippery slope and it may damage our characters.

The French romantic poet, Alphonse de Musset wrote a play called *Lorenzaccio*. In it the hero joins in the vices of Lorenzo de Medici, the ruler of Florence, in order to have the opportunity to kill him. But he becomes too corrupted to achieve any moral purpose. He says: "The evil I put on as a garment is now attached to my skin".

Every repressive dictator and his followers persuade themselves that they are torturing and killing in the interest of the people. They are really protecting their corruptly gained wealth and power. We are good at deluding ourselves.

Means affect ends. It is dangerous to do evil hoping for good. It will have a bad effect on us and reduce our capacity to do good overall. It would be wrong to torture a child to make his father reveal where the bomb was hidden. What sort of person would you become, if you did? Using wrong means also sets a bad example to others.

> Bandits capture you while you are backpacking in Peru. The local mafia boss is about to shoot forty peasants for not paying him his yearly tribute. He honours you as a representative of superior democratic values by offering to spare thirty, if you will personally shoot ten. Should you kill and save or refuse and let die? [9]

You would need the wisdom of Solomon and the foreknowledge of a prophet to know what to do. But you do have to consider the effect on others of becoming executioner to the bandit. Will it in the end promote happiness?

Sometimes the good end outweighs the bad means so much that it is obvious that we must use those means. If a pregnancy is going to kill the mother and with it her baby, then clearly abortion is necessary, however wrong you might think it to be usually. If a woman has an ectopic pregnancy, an injection must be given to kill the foetus and stop her dying. It is plain silly to insist that the woman's tube be removed with the foetus just so that technically one action does both good and bad.

I heard on the radio the story of a woman, whose daughter had the mind of a three-month-old infant. So that the girl would not grow too big for her to cuddle on her lap, nurse at home, and take about with her, she prevailed on the doctors to treat her with oestrogen to limit growth and to remove the breast buds and the uterus to avoid menstruation.

That would be a horrendous thing to do usually but in the circumstances it was entirely right, because it benefited the child and was unlikely to lead to any more questionable practices.

But there are some things that we should not do, however beneficial they are, because they are intrinsically so wicked that they can never be justified whatever the overall gain in human happiness.

Psychopathic serial murderers enjoy what they do. Such men, which they usually are, have healthy hearts, livers, lungs and kidneys. Each of these organs could save the life of a decent human being. Yet we know that it would be wrong to kill them to take their organs. Nor may we kill miserable, ungrateful grandpa to distribute the old miser's wealth among his needy grandchildren.

It is not a principle, which we must always follow, it is a warning that we are treading on dangerous ground when we transgress it.

12

Religious Duty Or General Happiness?

People rely mostly on one of two moral systems when they are thinking of their own happiness and of how they should treat others. Religion concentrates on doing the right thing, even if it does not make us or others happy. Utilitarianism concentrates on producing happiness and bothers less about how it is done.

Often there is agreement between these two approaches. The religious believe that their way is the best path to human happiness. Utilitarians accept that the safest path to human happiness is usually obedience to the moral law as enjoined by most religions. Both largely agree on which moral principles bind us. Moderates, who take either view, will usually work out agreements.

Nevertheless it is sometimes necessary to make a choice. Either we stick to principles whatever the result, as religious people may do or discard principles and try to make everyone happy, like a good utilitarian. We must choose between happy ends and good means. In this messy world compromise is the best answer. The religious person should accept that a particular commandment should not be obeyed when obedience to it will cause misery. The utilitarian should realise that it is very dangerous to flout important moral principles even in the hope of promoting happiness. When you do not know what to do for the best, the best thing is to do the right thing; it is the action most likely to turn out for the best.

The difference between the two approaches is that for one the moral law is the end in itself, our purpose in life. For utilitarians obedience to that law is just the means by which human happiness is secured. They accept that we risk damaging both ourselves and others in the long run when we do not obey it. But when it seems necessary they will sacrifice moral principle to maximise happiness. Those, who give priority to the moral law, will obey it at the expense of the general happiness.

There is always danger in a readiness to use bad means to attain good ends. Communist States perpetrated terrible evils to create a workers' paradise. But countries where religious fundamentalists are in control can be equally unhappy. Excessive loyalty to any institution, secular or religious, is dangerous. Its officials may concentrate on the good of the institution, not on the needs of those whom it is meant to serve. The logic is that it is right to sacrifice the individual on behalf of the many served by the organisation. This approach can seduce the religious as well as the secular. In Europe and North America church hierarchies have protected paedophiles and even allowed them to continue harming children to protect the reputation of the institution. In totalitarian countries new born babies have been stolen from mothers deemed unworthy so that they could bring happiness to worthy parents.

Who is right? Both and neither are. Sometimes we have to fudge a moral principle to avoid causing misery. Thus lies are sometimes necessary. On the other hand an action can be so evil that we should refuse to do it, however much happiness it brings to people. Big audiences enjoyed watching gladiators fight to the death in Rome. Such spectacles would probably be popular today but they would be wrong. Even if they did not brutalise society and damage happiness in the long run, they would still be intrinsically wrong. Severe cruelty is just wrong whatever might be gained from it. It is hardly surprising that no particular approach to how we should live has the monopoly of the truth.

It is impossible to decide in advance when moral principle and when happiness should take priority. Particular situations must be assessed on their merits. I argue for the primacy of happiness in general. Care for other people must manifest mainly by making them happy. The whole point of a moral law is that it promotes care for others. It is difficult to see the point of a moral principle, if it has no purpose beyond itself. If a moral principle does not in general promote happiness, why respect it? Presumably God had some purpose in imposing the moral law, the happiness of his creatures.

Religion makes us happy

Does religion make us happy? Yes it usually does. Does it help us to make others happy? Sadly it can deceive us into making them unhappy. Religion has four aspects; belief, ritual, community and morality. Ritual and a sense of community usually promote happiness by providing occupation and company.

People must find religion a benefit because it is popular in wealthy societies, like the US and in in poor countries, like Egypt. Religious people just seem to be happier in general than those without religion. Nevertheless religion has declined sharply in the West. Educated people no longer even recognise biblical quotations. Science has replaced God as the explanation for how it all came about. Political correctness has pushed religious teaching out of the schools. Religion is about duty and the modern ethos is one of personal rights.

The rituals of religion bring psychological benefit to the believer and they fulfil an important human need. They offer us an ordered way of life. They mark birth, marriage and death, the major milestones of our lives and those of our loved ones. They offer occupation and celebration when all is going well and distraction and comfort at times of distress. The joint observance of ritual promotes fellowship and community support both when we celebrate and when we grieve. Meeting together for ritual, communal worship promotes communal cohesion. So rituals benefit all and if they make any individual happier, the benefit spreads to the wider community.

Belief can help in several ways. We do not all face the prospect of extinction with equanimity. There is comfort in the belief that we have immortal souls, which will return to God, and that death is not the final parting from those we love. So our happiness in this world is increased by belief in future, eternal happiness in another world. Our bodies and our brains will return to the elements, from which they came but our souls, whatever they are, will earn the reward of our beliefs and actions in this world. Whether or not the belief is true is irrelevant to the comfort it brings.

The soul must be a thinking thing without material substance, like God, if it survives the destruction of the brain. There are two false claims that the mind or soul can be shown to do so. The first is the hocus-pocus of spiritualism, a sad combination of a mercenary desire to deceive and an emotional need to be deceived. The other is the nonsense talked about near death experiences.

If souls exist, do animals have them, and will Rover wag his tail, when you meet him again in heaven? If dogs have souls, then why should not frogs have souls? Where do you draw the line? If only humans have souls, then who was the first early human granted one, denied to his parents? The answer must be that both moral responsibility and the capacity to enjoy reward vary.

Belief in the soul and belief in God usually go together but Buddhists believe in souls, without believing in God. We can also believe in God without expecting to survive death.

Moral uncertainty troubles us and religion is the guide for many as we stumble through the moral jungle. Our duties are revealed in a holy book. A body of traditional, holy wisdom fills the gaps in revelation. Holy men give specific advice on difficult questions. So there is no need to worry or think too deeply about doing what is right. Religion is a refuge for those, who cannot face the inevitable uncertainties of this world.

After vacillating between Anglicanism and Catholicism the poet John Dryden (1631-1700) settled for Catholicism, an authoritarian religion. However, this extract from his poem smacks somewhat of abandoning his own moral sense given him by God.

> Rest then, my soul from endless anguish freed;
> Nor sciences thy guide, nor sense thy creed.
> Faith is the best ensurer of thy bliss. [1]

Religion also answers our need for spirituality and a sense of holiness. Karl Marx recognised that the injustice the common man suffers in this world increases the need for religion. He said something about religion, widely misunderstood today, because opiate use was then a rich man's pleasure.

> Religion is the sigh of the oppressed creature, the heart of a heartless world, just as it is the spirit of an age without spirit. It is the opium of the people. [2]

Religion can give to undistinguished people – that means almost all of us - the feeling that we are special to God, even if we cannot excel in the eyes of this world.

> Everyone must have two pockets, so that he can reach into one or the other, according to his needs. In his right pocket are to be the words: "For my sake was the world created," and in his left: "I am earth and ashes." [3]

Prayer

It is so widely practised that it must be good for us. It promotes happiness by supporting us in stress, giving us peace, comfort and uplift. It helps others by fortifying our good intentions.

It can take several forms. Hume said of prayers of praise: "It is an absurdity to believe that the Deity has human passions, and one of the lowest human passions, a restless appetite for applause." [4] But praising God fulfils a need to express gratitude for the good things in life, which we cannot take for granted, because: "destruction wasteth at noonday". [Psalm 91] There is also a duty to remember that some of us are more fortunate than others.

Petitions are essentially selfish.

Ask God, O man for neither that nor this;
Ask anything and that thine idol is. [5]

They can also be foolish. The old saying is that, when the gods wish to destroy us, they answer our prayers. Petitions tell God, who knows how it is, how it seems to me, as if he did not know that too. The benefit of petitionary prayer lies in the comfort it brings, not any other effect it causes.

The beautiful 23rd psalm, which begins: "The Lord is my shepherd" is an extended petition. In eleven lines it uses the first person singular pronoun seventeen times. It makes clear to God what you expect, and how you would like to thumb your nose at your enemies: "Thou preparest a table before me in the presence of mine enemies." Beauty is neither truth nor goodness, whatever Keats said. We are all very easily and understandably seduced by it.

Prayers can also be intercessions on behalf of others. That is admirable but there is no evidence of their efficacy. Their rationale is again that they give comfort, when neither we nor anyone else can help someone close to us in danger or distress.

Prayer can help when in moral doubt. It is not just talking to yourself, although the electrical activity in the brain may be the same as when you do talk to yourself. It is like bouncing your problem off someone else, instead of just ruminating on it. It is like practising your speech aloud in front of a mirror. But it is never a direct line to God.

This brings us to aspirations, when we pray to improve ourselves morally. Augustine (354-430), an important early Christian philosopher, said:

> "Why am I giving you an account of all these things? Not, obviously that you should learn them from me; but I excite my own love for you." [6]

He also said: "Lord, make me chaste but not yet." Why not enjoy a lifetime of sin and then secure eternal bliss by final repentance? Religion will always be popular.

Agnostics can also pray. The rational agnostic can be an emotional theist. Placebos help the patient even when he really knows that they contain no active drug. It can help to act as though we believe even when we do not. Julian Huxley, an atheist biologist, speaking of the future, said:

> There will be no room for petitionary prayer, much value in prayer involving aspiration and self-exploration" [7]

Agnostics also want to improve themselves morally and will use any helpful avenue to do so, of which prayer is one. They can treat God as a metaphor for their highest aspirations. They can pray in church in the company of other secret atheists, using the language of religion, which gives prayer its emotional resonance. The point of prayer is that it comforts and improves us, not that it has some effect on other entities. In any congregation there will be different levels of faith. There are more than a few agnostics in pulpits. Losing your faith is no reason to lose your job. Why should the agnostic not enjoy hymns and prayers, a sense of holiness, and companionship? Perhaps humanist groups need liturgies, rituals, creeds, hymns, and churches.

Religion can make you unhappy

Its dictates can be unhelpful. There is the absurdity of expecting loving couples to abstain from sexual relations to avoid producing unwanted children or infecting a partner with AIDS. It causes unnecessary guilt about loving, faithful homosexual relations. Some interpretations of religion teach that women are inferior to men and want to impose unjust restrictions on half the human race. It can also ask too much of us.

> My father left school very young and he asked his mother for his tea when he came home from work. She was very poor and very pious. She told him that she had given it to a poor man, who knocked on the door. He was hostile to religion ever after.

Your religion can make others happy

Most religions are reasonable guides to how we should treat other people, if interpreted sensibly, adapted to modern conditions, and overridden, when reason tells us that their dictates are clearly not good. Atheists have no guidance from scripture or priest but they are influenced by religious culture and can follow the moral principles of religion. Both the believer and the atheist should make moral decisions with humility and doubt and be ready to review them, when results are unsatisfactory. There is no honest escape from moral doubt.

All men of goodwill, believers or not, can hope to agree on the best way to care and promote happiness in our world. Just two things matter. The first is the wisdom, with which we decide how to care and the second is the strength of our determination to do it. Perhaps the moderate believer, who looks objectively at consequences, has a slight edge. Also we tend to behave better if we think we are being watched, whether by a policeman or by God.

Caring for others just because we think we should is a more noble part than doing so in the hope of posthumous reward. But others are not usually very interested in why you are helping them. They just want you to help them more and are delighted with whatever makes you do that. A sincere religion, short of fanaticism, can help us to do the right thing and persist in it against inclination. Do it for God, not for his ungrateful creature. Perhaps a little fear of God is no bad thing, even if belief is mistaken. And moderate believers put the happiness of others before counterintuitive dictates of their religion. They do not forbid the population of countries which suffer from famine or AIDS to use condoms. Care comes before dogma.

It has been said that, if you do not serve God, you will serve other masters. The decline in conventional religion has spawned a multitude of cults. Some are bizarre and some are crazy and vicious, as when a charismatic, evil "messiah" leads his followers to mass suicide. The cults also provide fellowship and direction, often from a bearded guru with feet of clay, and a fleet of limousines. All cults are dangerous substitutes for the major religions, although the major religions started as cults followed by the few until they became main stream. Nevertheless the probability that any particular cult will flourish is small. If a cult attracts us, we should ask ourselves questions. Will it make me happier? Will it help me to make others happier? Does it openly offer its doctrines and practices to public criticism? Can it defend them rationally? Would I have looked at them with suspicion before I got involved?

It is easier to teach our children to care about the happiness of others through religion than without it. Morality is easier to explain by modelling it on the nuclear family, supported by the wider family. By extension we are all brothers and sisters watched over by a stern but loving parent, whom we call God, upstaged by Santa in the festive season. We want our children to believe as we do and belief comes easily to us, when we are young, because we think of God as another loving, if more remote, father.

I see no objection to imposing your own religion on the child you bring up. You have him vaccinated and educated in his interest and without his informed consent. Anyway religious instruction gives him something to rebel against in adolescence. Children benefit from having a religion to reject and we have a duty to accept their rejection. [13] Also they may shed the belief but the moral compass is part of them and they will probably be happier for it.

Your religion can make others unhappy

Is belief or disbelief the better basis for caring? Virginia Woolf, in her novel *Mrs Dalloway*, refers to: "the atheist's religion of doing good for the sake of goodness. And of course she enjoyed it immensely." That just about sums it up. We feel we should care and making others happy makes us happy.

If religion provides the stronger impulse to caring, agnosticism exposes us to less danger of error. The agnostic may act according to a principle but when he sees that he is causing harm he does something different, which may be motivated by a different principle. His approach to morality has something in common with the approach of the scientist to the explanation of the natural world. The scientist proposes a theory about the way the world behaves. When observations show that it is incorrect he abandons it. Consequences also make the moderate believer change his mind.

On the other hand a Nobel prize-winning scientist said:

Religion is an insult to human dignity. With or without it, you'd have good people doing good things and evil people doing evil things. But for good people to do evil things it takes religion. [8]

But distinguished scientists, with the arrogance of eminence, sometimes pontificate in fields where they are more ignorant than the rest of us. In contrast champion athletes know perfectly well that fitness for one sport is not transferable to others.

Is religion actually responsible for most of the evil in the world? The terrible things that happened in the last century were not caused by religion. Unrestrained nationalism caused the world wars. Nazism and Stalinist communism were godless creeds, which killed people by the ten million. Mao was not thinking of religion when he launched his Cultural Revolution. Pol Pot had his own crazy ideas of political purification. The troubles in Northern Ireland were caused by tribalism, not religion as are many of the current genocides in Africa.

> A 14-year old girl was walking to school in Kandahar, Afghanistan. Two motorcyclists stopped her and asked where she was going. When she told them they sprayed her face with acid and asked her whether she was going to school now.

They were motivated by sadism, criminality and misogyny, not by religion.

No consequence however bad can make the fanatic, religious or secular, change his mind. The fanatics agree only with those, whose fanaticism is identical to their own. Religious conversion can be a pathway to fanaticism. It can be a refuge for those unable to endure the uncertainty which we should accept as our lot. Conversion on marriage to maintain family harmony is fine, but otherwise there is a case for sticking to the religion, which you grew up with. Most religions are fine, if taken in moderation. However, on a less serious note fanatics can also be ludicrous.

> A professor of rheumatology devoted a small part of his research budget to the investigation of alternative medicine. As many joint diseases are chronic and subject to episodes of improvement and deterioration, the field is rife with bogus cures. So it was a sensible and broadminded attitude. His assistant told the story that a man hobbled into the clinic, sat down with great pain, and told him that God had cured his arthri-

tis through prayer. The lecturer agreed to investigate the efficacy of prayer in his particular condition. But the professor blew his top, and pronounced the man a charlatan. Apparently the patient belonged to a different fundamentalist sect to the professor.

Is religion more likely than other ideologies to make good people do bad things? Most of the people, who do terrible things on a grand scale, think they are acting morally. Good people were inclined to deny the evils of Stalinism and betray their own nation, because communism had seduced them. The Nazis and all the genocidal murderers persuade themselves that they have no duty of care to humans with other ethnicities or nationalities. Any ideological denial of truth can make men, who are otherwise good, act wickedly. Fanaticism of any sort is harmful, whether the fanatics are religious, animal rights zealots or deluded conspiracy theorists. Whenever we hold to a belief against reason, compassion, common sense or the evidence of our eyes, we are in grave moral danger.

All fanatical faiths, whether religious or secular, refuse to entertain doubt. The believer is sure he is right and especially that his own religion or his own secular ideology is absolutely right. In the case of religion the claim is that God has given mankind one genuine revelation. Believers maintain this with passion. They are untroubled that millions of other believers maintain just as passionately that some other book contains the sole, genuine revelation, not theirs. The believers only make assertions and never present any evidence.

The religious should remember that it is the sin of spiritual pride to be sure that you are right and you know God's wishes better than the adherents of other religions. "No counsel can be given on how to break pride. We must struggle with it all the days of our life." [9] Believers should pray, hope and even think that they are right, as long as they accept that they may be wrong. The fact that co-religionists have been morally wrong in the past should shake their certainty that the current dictates of the faith must be right now. Equally how can you be sure that your secular ideology is right and that other views held with equal passion are wrong? How can any humans be infallible? Moderation and compromise in religion and politics achieve the best results. The fanatics, both religious and secular, destroy the world; only the caring moderates, both religious and secular, can repair it.

There are many religions, each with their different moral instructions. They do not agree how many wives a man should have. They disagree about the permissibility of abortion. Within sects there are fierce debates about whether women or homosexuals may be priests. How can you know that yours is the true religion? It is pure chance that you were born into a Hindu, not a Muslim family. After all you might have been switched at birth because of a mistake at the hospital. What if you had been kidnapped as a child?

> In 1858 a Jewish boy, Edgardo Mortara, was forcibly taken from his parents by the papal authorities because a Christian maid had secretly baptised him when he was ill. He grew up to be a happy Christian monk. He might equally have become a pious rabbi, if he had not been kidnapped. Whether or not the kidnap saved his soul is a matter of opinion. [10]

Obedience to religious authority is a second source of moral danger and cause of harm to others. There is something less than human about handing the rationality and moral sense, which you believe that God gave you, to another imperfect human. It is an abnegation of responsibility to submit your own heart and brain to the dictates of someone else, however apparently holy. It is moral laziness. We should always listen to advice but in the last resort we have the responsibility to decide ourselves. It is sinful to abandon reason, common sense, and compassion to any authority, whether secular or religious.

Blind obedience is also given to secular authority, including that of the white coat and it can be just as dangerous.

In a famous experiment one group of students was asked to administer electric shocks to a second group behind a glass screen. The first group were assured by white-coated, respected teachers that the second group were volunteers. They were exhorted to continue, even when the shocks appeared to cause considerable distress to the students behind the screen. This they nearly all did. The shocks were sham; the distress was simulated; the first group were the experimental subjects. [11]

Utilitarianism

It has two planks, the hedonistic and the egalitarian. It claims that actions are good, when they cause pleasure and bad, when they cause distress, so it emphasises consequences not principles of conduct. Unlike the classical hedonism of Epicurus, it values the happiness of others, as well as our own. If to act morally is to confer benefit, and if the main benefit we can confer is happiness, then utilitarianism captures most of morality. It is good to spread happiness and fortunately doing good makes most of us happy. Because it is egalitarian, everyone counts as one and no one as more or less than one. Serf and sovereign are equal in moral importance and that seems right.

However, there are major problems with both planks of the system. Not everyone will accept that happiness is the supreme good, although I have tried to make a strong case that it is. But the problem of means and ends remains. We know how we are acting but not what we will achieve. We cannot be sure of all the consequences of our actions and it would be absurd even to try to guess them most of the time. In practice we are more likely to promote happiness by following moral principles and letting the results take care of themselves. That is rule-utilitarianism but it is still utilitarianism. Our goal remains happiness and we allow ourselves to break the rules when the advantage in doing so seems clear.

The egalitarian aspect of utilitarianism is also flawed. Action cannot be decided simply on the total amount of happiness it will produce irrespective of who is made happy. Egalitarianism conflicts with the duty to respect moral proximity. Can everyone really count for me as one? What if I must choose between saving my brother or two strangers? My mother will have something to say, if I choose the strangers, and it will not need her to make me unhappy. Should I support cancer care in my own country or save more lives by helping to avert starvation in a distant land? Should I care for horses as much as people? And does someone, to whom I owe a debt of gratitude, not deserve my special consideration? We must weigh the amount of good we could do but also consider to whom we are doing it. Such decisions are subjective and we hope to have enough wisdom not to go too badly wrong in any direction. It can be wrong to give too much weight to moral proximity. The judge must be impartial between his friend and a stranger.

When a single miner is trapped underground we spend millions to save his life, although that money could be used to save many more lives, if we left him. We save him for the two reasons why simplistic utilitarianism does not work. We are morally closer to him than to unknown people, whose lives might be saved. If we left him, the moral fabric of our society would change.

PART II

Feeling Happier About Tough Moral Decisions

13

Tackling Decisions

M ost of us are happier when we feel that we have done the right thing but how do we know what is right?

Backward moral thinking

We make most of our moral decisions backward. We follow our intuitions and then find reasons to justify them. Usually that is inevitable because it is impossible to puzzle over every decision and it is fine because the heart is often right.

Unfortunately intuition sometimes deserts us leaving us perplexed and unhappy. It can mislead us and cause us grief later. The heart is not always wise, as the song says. It is some-times an excuse for doing what suits us when a little thought would tell us it was wrong. Once we make an intuitive decision we are tempted to see only the facts, which justify it. We bias our prediction of the consequences of the action required by intuition to suit that intuition. We persuade ourselves that in the situation only one principle is relevant. My duty to send my children to private schools enjoins me to embezzle from my employer.

We also find that others have just as strong an intuition as we do but entirely different. I think nurses should be paid more than stockbrokers but you disagree. How can we know who is right? Disputes between people with different moral intuitions generate so much emotion that no one can consider the issue rationally. It can be like the deaf shouting at the deaf or the blind making rude gestures to the blind. Facts and predictions are proclaimed without evidence. One principle or one objective is given priority over others with no attempt at justification. When we commit ourselves emotionally we are in the grip of aggravated backward moral thinking.

Moral doubt is the lot of honest people and disagreement with others is the lot of everyone. Even in retrospect we will not agree on what was the right action nor, if we are honest with ourselves, be sure that our own judgement was right. Nevertheless, we have to make decisions in the face of uncertainty and we have to discuss disagreements. Even if there is no single moral truth in the world, there may be a best way to discover what is not true.

Forward moral thinking

Only stepwise forward thinking can clarify our own thoughts and enable us to discuss problems rationally with those, who disagree with us. It is a four-step process. The first step is the determination of the facts of the situation. The second step looks at the consequences of different possible actions. For the third step we assemble all the principles relevant to the situation and the objectives, which they require, which in turn determine the action we take. Honesty tells us that we must carefully consider principles and objectives, which support actions, which we reject. How else can we meaningfully engage with others? The fourth step determines the action to be taken by choosing between objectives. That is when agreement usually breaks down. Each principle has a different importance for different people. You value honesty and I value kindness more. So you want to tell him a painful truth but I do not. Nor do we give the same importance to the objectives, which we derive from each principle. You do not think he will find the truth so painful but I think he will.

There is a theoretical advantage to stepwise, forward thinking. Suppose that you wanted to explain a moral dispute here on Earth to a Martian. He is a rational, social creature as we are, the mythical ideal observer, prepared to put his own worldview to one side and understand ours. He would judge our behaviour as we would that of a troop of chimpanzees. He may not exist but we can invent him. How could you explain and justify action on Earth to him other than by a four-step, forward analysis?

The real practical advantages of forward thinking are important. It clarifies our own thoughts. It is the best way to discuss disputes, because it establishes areas of agreement and isolates disagreements for focussed attention.

THE STEPS

I will illustrate the four steps by looking at how we would explain a specific action to our Martian. A passer-by seizes a man about to kill himself by jumping off a bridge. How do we justify this gross interference with the liberty of another?

> **Step I.** The situation - The man is standing on the parapet and is clearly going to jump to his death. We do not know why he intends to do this.
> **Step II.** Consequences - A passer-by stops him forcibly. The action preserves his life, at least temporarily. The consequence of inaction would be his death.
> **Step III** Principles - On the one hand there is the duty to save life. Opposing this is the duty to respect the autonomy of a rational adult.
> **Step IV.** Choosing between objectives - The Martian reasonably asks why we do not put respect for autonomy first and let the man jump.

So we give a fuller account of the situation. The rescuer knows that those, who jump off bridges, often have a depressive illness and their life situation may not justify suicide. The man may be unable to make a competent decision, so seizing him does not constitute disrespect to his autonomy. You would need to explain what a depressive illness is to the Martian, because on his happy planet depression is unknown.

He is still not satisfied. He thinks it more likely that the man had taken a rational, considered decision to end his life to avoid a situation worse than death. Perhaps public shame was about to reduce his happiness level. On Mars life seems pointless without perfect happiness. It is right there to kill yourself both to maintain the high average Martian level of happiness and to avoid public shame. Indeed people used to kill themselves to avoid public shame here on Earth.

We answer this interplanetary condemnation. First we point to the situational difference. We accept on Earth that life is quite unsatisfactory at times and many rational earthlings struggle on in the hope of improvement. Depressive illness is common on Earth. We suspect that the man is depressed, but we cannot be sure, because we lack Martian telepathy. We are not as wise as the Martians and impulsive suicide is not unknown here. People, who kill themselves, would later regret having done so, if their action had not made regret impossible. Also public figures in our indulgent countries rebound rapidly after disgrace. Indeed they come out of prison telling us how the experience has made them even worthier of our admiration than they told us that they were before. If he jumps off the bridge, he can never change his mind but if we stop him, he can always jump off another bridge. Fortunately Martians understand probability and irreversibility.

Our Martian agrees that the situations are different on the two planets; in different situations identical principles give different answers. But we still have a dispute about the relative importance of two moral principles, respect for autonomy and respect for life. Martians would never disrespect someone's autonomy, if there were the remotest chance that he was rational. But we might chance it to save life. So we still disagree, but we understand each other now and mute our mutual criticism. We even realise why each of us has come to have different values. We are not seeking universal moral truths. We are trying to work out in each situation the right thing to do and the best thing to do, fortunately often the same. We do this by discovering as many facts as possible and considering all relevant principles.

I will now look at the steps in more detail starting with the current facts and then the consequences, the new facts, which action will produce.

Step I; The situation.

Normative ethical analysis involves the application of moral principles to specific situations. Hume said: "all the objects and all their relations to each other must be known before we can approve an action." We need the facts to make every kind of decision, not just moral decisions. Obviously we rarely do know all the facts, but there is a duty to find out as many as possible.

Chance often determines if we make good or bad decisions, whether we are gambling on the stock exchange or thinking about the morally correct course of action. There are not just the facts, which we do not know before we act; there are the unexpected facts which emerge, and events, which occur after we have taken action. Events occur, which no one foresees. In retrospect was it wise to build nuclear power stations in areas of Japan at risk from earthquakes and tsunamis?

So there is such a thing as moral luck. You appear to have done the right thing if all turns out well and the wrong thing when it goes badly. We have to forgive ourselves when we unintentionally do more harm than good, whether through mischance or misjudgement.

A woman was dying of cancer. She had long ago left her son with learning disability in an institution and had lost contact with him. She felt a strong need to see him again before she died. Unfortunately he had already died. Her doctor and the director of the orphanage deceived her. They substituted a boy of the same age. Mother and supposed son spent a happy day together, and the woman felt much peace, when she found her son well cared for. The "son" also had a pleasant day out with the woman. Two people benefited from the deception but what if the woman had found out? The doctor and the director lied and were lucky. [1]

Situations may change during the course of a series of decisions. A change in a situation changes the effect of an action. What was good recently has now become bad. For example, many believe that it is more wrong to kill a foetus after it is viable outside the womb than before it becomes viable. Foetuses are now viable earlier because medical science has advanced. An abortion at twenty-four weeks now kills a human possibly capable of happy life outside the womb, whereas previously it did not. Therefore the moral argument against killing it has become stronger. Indeed it has resulted in a change in U K law.

Our personal moral outlook affects our appreciation of a situation. We do not believe what we see; we see what we believe, because that is what we expect to see. We must try to avoid selective blindness to facts inconsistent with our fixed beliefs. Theft is wrong but it is also wrong to refuse to consider the circumstances of the thief. When those, who disagree with us on a moral issue, bring facts to our notice, which call our judgement into question, there is a duty to test them and then, if necessary, review our judgement.

Often we must acknowledge that we do not possess all the important facts. So then parties to a moral dispute should accept that, when more facts emerge, their opponents might yet prove right. But we have to make decisions now, not in ten years' time when more will be known. We will disagree but bitterness is less when all acknowledge that necessary facts are lacking, making any judgement provisional. There is a duty to accept the possibility that new, unexpected information may show that he, who we see as a fool, may yet prove right. Hostility is less, if we start by confining ourselves to facts and set values aside. Stepwise analysis can make discussion start more sensibly.

Step II; Consequences of action

Two laws of nature control our lives; one is cause and effect; the other is probability. If we take an action, it will have an effect. The effect is never certain, only almost certain, probable or quite uncertain. It is often also quite unexpected. When we cross the road we predict we will reach the other side, but sometimes we prove wrong. Nevertheless we have to try to predict all the facts which will result from different proposed actions in a situation. So the logical next step, when deciding what to do, is to try to predict all the consequences of any action considered in a situation.

We have to consider the unwanted as well as the wanted consequences of the action, the objective and the side effects of achieving it or trying to. Our duty is to make the best predictions we can. We must rely on probability and we need luck. If we do not have it, what seemed right turns out disastrously.

> You are walking in the street when a man stops his car and asks you for directions. It is a simple, minor good deed to tell him, which we do at no cost and with little thought. How can we know that he is a contract killer looking for his victim?

It is even harder to predict the extended effects of an action, the consequences of the consequences. We must consider the good or bad effect, which helping Smith may have on Jones, the effect of the effect. Making my friend happy makes my friend's friend's friend a little happier. Effects ripple out. A woman has to consider the cost to her existing children of preserving the life of her unborn baby. How can you predict extended effects? You can't; you can only do your best.

Consequences are often incommensurable. To take a medical example, doctors have two important objectives, the prolongation of life and the reduction of distress. Anyone, who has two goals, knows that sometimes they may conflict. When chemotherapy is considered, it may be hard to weigh the chance of prolongation of life against the damage to quality of life which drugs cause. It is for the doctor to supply the best available information, the possible consequences of the proposed actions. But different people are in different situations and also weigh different consequences differently; so one answer will not suit all. The Golden Rule is oriented to the one affected by the action. The patient must choose the mix of risks, benefits and harms, which suit him best. He must balance the importance of different consequences for himself. Others can advise but cannot do it for him. Moral duty will be involved for some. If I think that I have a duty to prolong my life as much as possible, I might endure distress, which most others would think not worthwhile.

We must avoid confusing disputes about consequences with disputes about principles. Control of the sale of alcohol, cigarettes, and other drugs is a consequential, not a moral issue. It is an argument about how we can best improve the health of the public and reduce crime. The Americans prohibited the sale of alcohol and it promoted crime. Only consequential considerations should apply to control of the sale of any drug.

The use of these substances is a moral issue for the individual, not for the community. Even for the individual the morality of their use turns solely on the effect they will have on his capacity to help or harm others. Humans have always sought what might be called a chemical vacation from the rigours of life. The ascetic may condemn this but perhaps the ordinary person needs his holiday, especially now that religion is no longer a solace. But we are always keen to denounce the pleasures and vices which do not appeal to us.

It is hard to know how much good or harm criminalisation or legalisation of a particular addictive drug would do. If we recognise that it is a dispute about consequences, not principles, debate about these matters will generate more light and less heat.

> When scientists discover a mummified body of archaeological or historical importance, they subject it to extensive investigation. They x-ray it, endoscope it, cut off bits for various analyses and then they display it to a curious public. If the person, who once inhabited that body, were able to protest against this disrespect, he would certainly do so vigorously. Until recently no one has seen any moral problem about this practice.

We would be appalled if this were done to the body of someone recently deceased. There was an outcry in the UK, when the public discovered that pathologists retained the organs of dead children for later study, in the hope of advancing medical science to benefit other children. People felt strongly that parents should be informed of what was proposed, and should have the right of refusal.

Now neither recently dead children nor long dead mummies can suffer anything, so what is the difference? It is this; in the case of mummies, there is no one to suffer emotional distress, when they learn of the desecration of a body. No one alive today loved Tutankhamen. Ancient Egyptians, bodies in bogs, and prehistoric men in ice seem morally distant from us. But people are very unhappy, if they feel that the bodies of their loved ones are not treated with respect. It is their unhappiness we consider. Disrespect for the dead is less important than distress to the living.

Participants in an ethical dispute will disagree about the likelihood of different consequences. Most people will have taken an intuitive stand before even thinking about the issue. So they will inevitably bias their assessments of the probability and importance of consequences to support their moral preconceptions. That is our usual backward moral thinking. And even agreed principles give different answers, when predicted consequences are different. The right action depends on the situation that is and on the one that will come about. However, bias is less likely if facts are considered before and separately from values and principles, which we try to put temporarily out of mind. It is easier to agree about facts than about values, and easier to demonstrate the consequences of following a principle than to agree on the moral importance of doing so. Disputes about facts are difficult enough but hopefully less bitter than disputes about principles. Time may show who was right, although usually too late. And we will never know what would have happened, if we had done the other thing, because the stream of life flows only one way.

It is much more difficult when different actions are required by different moral principles. It is easier to be rational about facts than it is about values.

Step III; Principles

For the purposes of moral discussion it does not matter whether principles are universal. Meaningful discussion requires only that those in dispute agree that the principle and the objective indicated by it are valid and relevant to the situation.

But that leaves plenty of room for disagreement. To which principle should we give priority? Is the relief of distress more important than respect for the sanctity of life? What is the scope of the principle? Do we have a duty of beneficence to all animals, to all humans, or only to citizens of this country? How important is the objective it indicates in the situation? We respect the lives of both unborn babies and old men but are they of equal importance?

Validity and relevance

If you adduce a fact in a discussion, it must be true and relevant to the discussion. If you suggest that a moral principle should decide a course of action, then that principle must also be valid and relevant to the issue.

A moral principle may be entirely relevant, but many will question its validity. Thus the principle that "speciesism" is as wrong as racism implies that the suffering of a rat is of equal importance to the suffering of a human, assuming that the distress is equal. [1] This principle is relevant to experimenting on animals, to enjoying a nice steak, and to deciding whether to leave your money to the cats' home or the orphanage. However, most people, who wish to act morally, will regard the principle as not just invalid but ludicrous.

A moral principle may be perfectly valid, but when you think about it, you realise that it is irrelevant to the situation. The demands of a principle are limited to precisely what it specifies. The duty to tell the truth does not extend to those who would use the knowledge for evil purposes. Respect for life does not extend to the life of someone about to commit murder.

Take the situation of a woman contemplating an abortion, because she is pregnant after being raped. The woman has always believed that abortion is wrong, and now she finds herself in this terrible situation. When the issue was discussed on a television programme, a nun passionately declared that a foetus resulting from rape had just as much moral importance as one resulting from consensual intercourse.

Now the conviction, with which an opinion is held, bears little relation to its truth or moral value. Sometimes we affirm most passionately those facts and opinions about which we have some inner doubts. But even if a moral conviction is based on sound principle, that does not make it relevant to the situation. In this case the sentiment was genuine and the principle was valid. She was right that the objective of preserving life was of equal importance in both cases. But it is an argument, which knocks down a straw man. There is no claim that the life of the foetus has less moral value. The duty to preserve the life of a foetus is the same whether it is conceived after rape or by consensual intercourse in holy matrimony. So the passionate plea was irrelevant. The argument for easier abortion after rape is based on the distress the pregnancy causes the woman, her moral responsibility for the pregnancy, and the prospects of the foetus.

The advantages so far of forward analysis are as follows.

- It has helped us to take a more dispassionate view of the facts of the situation and the consequences of action, because we are not surrendering our principles.
- We realise that our moral adversary is not a rogue because he too is motivated by a moral principle, even if it is invalid, irrelevant or given undue weight.

Now I turn to choosing between objectives.

14

Making Decisions

We can look at the facts; we can predict what will happen, if we do this or do that and we can find a moral principle, which tells us to do one thing or the other. That does not help when different moral principles suggest different actions. We can't feed facts and principles into a computer and get an answer. We tend to rely on emotion, intuition, habit or holy instruction to choose. But even when we think we know what to do, other people think differently. However, there are ways of thinking clearly about making choices and discussing them more usefully.

Some will think that one principle always overrides another, whatever the objectives involved. Killing humans is wrong, even when the old man begs to die, because human life is sacred.

But most accept that no single moral principle can require total obedience in every situation. We can't avoid deciding when an objective, derived from one principle becomes more important than that derived from another principle, the tipping point. How much should I let my children suffer before I steal bread?

We all think that we exercise practical wisdom when making a choice, but it is inevitably personal and arbitrary, and therefore dispute is equally inevitable. Often the duty to perform a beneficent action demands a response different from the action required by some other principle. Thus the French existentialist novelist, Albert Camus (1913-1960), asked how much blood we should wade through to be right. How much misery should we cause for the sake of justice? Should we let the tyrant escape justice to save lives? In the end we want to make the choice with which we will feel happier, because we think it is the better choice.

Step IV: Choosing between objectives

There are some rational ways to approach the choice between objectives even when they come from different principles.

The scope of a principle may be limited. There are situations to which it does not apply. The life of someone about to murder another person is not sacred. One principle may modify the scope of another. It is wrong to kill. Accelerating death is slow killing. The double effect principle permits doctors to relieve distress even when it accelerates the death of a patient. Perhaps the current Pope had this principle in mind when he hinted that using a condom to avoid communicating HIV infection might be permitted, even though it prevented conception. But the prevention of conception would have to be an unwanted and unavoidable side effect.

Sometimes we just have to compromise between the demands of two principles. At some point the objective required by one outweighs that required by the other. For example hearts for transplantation are rationed. There are simply not enough donor hearts to go round. My personal right, like yours, is to the treatment, which will do me the most good, even if it will not do me all that much good. But doctors ought to do as much good as they can with the means available. A suggested resolution of this conflict of two principles is to give patients, who stand to gain at least a year of life with a treatment, an equal right to it with those who would live much longer [1]. The choice of one year is arbitrary but all compromises are arbitrary. As in politics agreement is better than war even at the cost of concession, but how much concession?

A third principle may decide a conflict between two other principles. There is a duty not to distress sentient beings. There is a duty to promote human welfare. In medical research these two duties may clash. A whole life principle may tip the balance. We must ensure that the overall life experience of any animal, which we use for any purpose, is good, even if periods of its life are not ideal. The application of this principle may decide whether a particular experiment is justified. We still make the decision by weighing objectives. How much distress can we let an animal suffer when we use it? How much would humans benefit from its suffering?

Several moral principles may combine to overrule an opposing one.

You are lying on a trolley in the emergency room of your local hospital. You are in distress and waiting to be admitted to the ward so that the nurses can make you comfortable and start your treatment. But the ward is full. One patient is taking a long time to die. It would be in the interest of all to give him a hefty dose of morphine. He is not comfortable; there is nothing more that he can do with his life; he wants to die; his relatives could start the funeral arrangements and you could have his bed.

The utilitarian principle tells us to reach for the syringe. But both the double effect principle and a version of Kant's categorical imperative tell us that the interests of one patient may not be served by killing another. Each person is an end in himself and must not be used solely as a means. Killing the bed blocker also violates the duty of care, the implicit promise, which a doctor gives to her patient that she will act only in his interest. Respect for life and respect for the law tell us not to do it. It is a slippery slope to killing other awkward patients. If one argument does not stop the killing, then another will.

MAKING THE CHOICE

Each action has an objective in view. We choose between objectives, not between the principles underlying them. Only fanatics stick to a principle regardless of all other considerations. I may hate to see animals suffer but I should not stop scientific research by injuring the scientist's children. Several factors affect the strength of the duty to achieve a moral objective.

Importance of the objective

The greater the benefit which we can confer, the greater is the duty to confer it. Is it life we could save or inconvenience we might prevent? I should break the law to save his life but not his money. The incommensurability of different benefits can make choice difficult even without the complication of other factors. A good start is to let those, whom we wish to help decide for themselves between different benefits. He must choose whether he wants his life longer or more comfortable. That is the Golden Rule. But often the agent, not the object, has to choose. Should I go to see another patient or come home to look after my family?

The importance of an objective may depend on the object of the action. All should be protected from harm but some may deserve more protection than others, because they suffer more from a similar harm. I should steal neither from the rich nor the poor but it is worse to steal from the poor, because they suffer more. I should save the lives of the young and the old but when forced to choose I should save the young. It is more important to save the many than the few, even at greater cost to myself.

Cost

We are entitled to consider how great a cost we will have to endure to confer a benefit. My right to happiness clashes with my duty. If the cost is trivial compared to the benefit, action is obligatory. We must leave off reading the newspaper and run to the water's edge to throw a lifebelt to a drowning man. We are not obliged to incur a cost as great as the benefit to him. I do not have to protect a stranger from bullets with my own body. I am a person of equal value to him. That would be an exemplary not an obligatory action. Of course there is a large gap between paying a trivial cost and paying an excessive cost. It is a personal decision, into which we must put all the criteria discussed here.

We should act as we wish others to act so we should ask of ourselves what we would expect of others, accepting that the widow's mite means more than the banker's millions. But how much could I ask of others? Saints and heroes suffer more cost to do good than can reasonably be expected of most of us. The saint puts the interests of others before his own. The hero risks more danger and suffering to do good than would the rest of us. We are neither.

Some avoid responsibility by claiming "a duty to myself". It is usually a dishonest way of refusing to pay the cost of performing a duty to others. We have only three duties to ourselves. We must forgive ourselves for our failures; we need not ask of ourselves more than we do of others; we must not neglect our health, because we cannot care for others, if we do.

Increased responsibility

We become more responsible for a situation than other people in several ways. If we have promised to benefit someone, the duty to do so becomes stronger. A broken promise is an aggravated lie, because someone is depending on what we said. Some promises are explicit. Implicit promises may be even more important, as in that of a parent to a child or a doctor to a patient. When the nuclear explosion occurs it is hard luck on the engineer who has to deal with it but that was the promise he made when he took the job.

We have increased responsibility for problems which we have knowingly caused. Clean up the mess which you made.

However, the politician, who starts the wrong war, should give place to one who can pursue it better or end it quicker.

Chance lands unexpected responsibility in your lap. If you are the only one to see the man drowning, then you have the duty to try to save him. When someone knocks on our door for help we probably wish that he had gone next door. But he came to us and we must try to help, inconvenient though it is.

Gratitude increases responsibility. If someone has helped us, especially at personal cost, we have an increased duty to help him. Social life is built on reciprocating favours. We owe to our parents, who have nurtured us, and to the benefactor, who befriended us. I should put myself out more for someone who has helped me, or who probably would help me, if necessary. I have less duty to unhelpful acquaintances. When Confucius was asked whether we should repay hostility with kindness, he replied: "How then do you repay kindness? Repay hostility with uprightness and repay kindness with kindness. " [2]

When we are more able than others to help there is an increased duty to do so. Our particular talents should serve us and serve others, whether it is a musical, an administrative or a nurturing talent. As we usually enjoy doing what we are good at, this particular enhancement of the duty to achieve a moral objective is less onerous than some others. Life is so much easier, when inclination assists duty. And there is a duty to make it easier for ourselves to perform good actions. Peter Singer, a contemporary philosopher, points out that you stay with it longer, if you enjoy it. He quotes the words of an admired friend.

I think one can be a lot more effective, if one really feels good about doing it, if one gets up in the morning just raring to pick up where one left off the night before – as opposed to doing it for others, doing it because it should be done, doing it because it just is the right thing to do. [3]

We may have to do good in distasteful ways but we do so much better and feel so much happier doing the good that we enjoy.

Moral proximity

In so far as responsibility is distant from us personally it is of less moral importance, but in so far as it is near to us, it is of more importance. We have an especial duty to help our kin, friends, and fellow citizens. It has been calculated that we can know personally only up to about one hundred and fifty people and presumably we have a greater responsibility to them than to those unknown to us.

In the modern world television has brought us morally nearer than we were to people in distant lands. We see their suffering. They no longer starve in far off countries, of which we know little. As individuals we cannot stop all the misery in the world but we can stop a little of it. When we have done what we should, it is of no benefit to those who remain in misery, to let guilt spoil our own enjoyment of life.

The danger of trying to care for all equally is that we will love some less rather than the many more. Worthy causes deluge us with requests for help, especially at Christmastime. There is little point giving small sums to hundreds of charities. It is sensible to confine support to those charities, to which we feel nearer for personal reasons, after deciding what fraction of our income should be given to charity. Moral proximity also demands spontaneous giving, either to the appeal which suddenly touches us, or to the beggar who excites our pity in the street. However, expect no gratitude from the gratified beggar. It is he, who has benefited you, by enabling you to perform a good deed.

Peter Singer noted that we would spoil an expensive pair of shoes in the mud to rescue someone, who we saw drowning. But we would not sell the shoes to save some one far away from starving. The difference is due to moral proximity and the chance, which has given us personal responsibility. We would spend millions of pounds to save a trapped miner, when that money could save more lives, if used in another way. But what would we be, if we did not feel moral proximity and let him die in order to do more good to unknown people? Sympathy must overcome utilitarian considerations or we become calculating machines, not fellow sufferers.

The recent rescue of the 33 Chilean miners is a case in point. It unified the nation in a good cause. The struggle and its successful outcome probably increased the general level of happiness in the country for a time. It probably made Chileans nicer to each other. The same effect can be produced by a trivial event, like a football match. Sadly war can also unite a nation in common effort and considerably reduce depressive symptoms in the population. Common goals unite whether or not they are worthy just as admirable qualities can be put to good or bad use.

Moral proximity should not overcome all other obligations; it must not become moral exclusivity. We have a responsibility for the wider world, as well as to the man next door. Moral proximity tells us to help our family and friends more than the stranger, but not to the exclusion of the stranger. Nepotism should not overrule justice. We want to appoint the son of a friend to the coveted post. That may mean injustice to the best person for the job and betrayal of the community, which entrusted us to find the person, who would serve it best.

The men and women of resistance movements in the Second World War were faced by a terrible dilemma. They had a duty to fight occupation on behalf of the nation. They had a duty to hide the fugitive. Yet often they were putting their own families at risk to do so. Moral proximity and communal duty were in conflict. Heroes rarely have a sophisticated knowledge of ethics. If we think of those who have resisted tyranny in large or small ways, they are usually people strongly moved by compassion or a sense of justice. Action comes from emotion, more than intellect.

The feminist ethic emphasises responsibility and moral proximity. It puts the individual in his trouble over abstract principles, which appeal more to men. [4] It puts the loving action before the right action. It is consistent with utilitarianism but discards its egalitarian aspect.

> A man asked a female friend with a very strong sense of right and wrong, if she would hide him, were he to commit a murder. She said that she would be very sad but she would do so.

Contrast this with the priority given by a man to public duty.

> Brutus, the head of the ancient Roman republic, had his two sons executed for plotting to restore the monarchy. David's painting (1789) shows him sitting in stern, impassive, grief as their bodies are borne home,

while the womenfolk lament.

The female brain is more proficient at communication, empathy and so is better at verbal and social skills. The male brain is better adapted to system analysis and spatial problems. So men think deeply and logically about what to do and come to wrong answers. Women can come up with the right answer without the need for prolonged thought. Naturally I exaggerate because the overlap is enormous. The new man is into childcare and domestic skills and can fortunately exercise the feminine side of his nature.

A feminist ethic focusses on the importance of our relationships with and responsibility for each other. It provides a valuable corrective to the moral coldness of principle based ethics. It is not a complete ethic, because always to do the loving thing over the right thing would lead to anarchy and injustice. Principle must sometimes overrule feeling. If the emphasis on moral proximity becomes excessive there is a risk of unjustifiable exclusions. Had the man embarked on serial murder his female friend would have had a clear duty to turn him in, however close their relationship. We have to choose between love and duty. Emotion is the mainspring of our action but reason must control it.

Reduced responsibility

Responsibility is reduced when it is shared. Tom reasonably asks himself why he should do more for the common good than others. John is so much richer than he is and has a greater obligation than he does in the particular situation. He does not wish to be Tom Fool. The answer is that he does what is right because that is what makes him happy or just because he thinks he ought, whereas John does not.

I have suggested some factors to consider when choosing between moral objectives. Consultation with those who we respect helps. Time for consideration helps. Systematic thought helps. Moral decisions can still be very difficult. We may never be happy about what we decide to do. When we have done our best we have to forgive ourselves for error.

Advantages of forward thinking

The logical sequence proposed combats moral preconceptions. We have to establish the current facts of a situation before we predict the facts which would result from actions which we might take. Even if we cannot agree about current facts, we might agree on what must be done to establish them. We will disagree about the likely consequences of different actions, but we know that the truth may emerge later. It is also easier to discuss consequences, when doing so implies no concession about principles.

The process can be fluid. Parties can agree that conclusions will be contingent on the ascertainment of facts or the observation of the results of action. If the legalisation of euthanasia damaged palliative care, then legalisation would have to be reconsidered. Unexpected and unwelcome consequences make us reconsider what we have done. [5]. We have to look again at all four steps of the decision process. Principles have meaning only when we apply them to cases. The results of applying them can make us reconsider our principles. If you find your well-meaning interference in the affairs of another ends in disaster, you have made a mistake. Perhaps you have given too much priority to conferring an uncertain benefit over respect for autonomy.

Different moral principles suggest different objectives, leading to different actions. We should look at all the relevant and valid moral principles before trying to choose between the actions they require. We can agree that an action, which we severely condemn, is nevertheless motivated by a valid and relevant moral principle. The dispute is about the priority of principles and objectives. This recognition encourages respect for an adversary as part of the same moral community. Those who disagree with us may be badly mistaken, but they are not wicked. Recognition of the validity and relevance of other people's principles has two further advantages. It reduces our certainty that we are obviously and absolutely right, while all others are wrong. It should make us regret that we are overriding a valid and relevant moral principle when we make our choice.

An approach to at least trying to make the choice between objectives rationally has been described and more may be impossible. However, forward, stepwise thinking might reduce moral disagreement a little, or more realistically clarify areas of agreement and points of disagreement. It is open to people of widely different moral outlooks and experience of the world.

There is nothing new about this four-step approach based on the application of values to facts. My intention is to emphasise that it is the best way for people with diverse worldviews to hold meaningful ethical discussions. For example it is the only way that a Martian could understand our disputes. It is the best way for anyone in moral doubt to tackle a problem. It might help those in dispute to understand and respect each other's views more and bring them a little closer to agreement.

Problems

An historical step has been ignored. The origin of a situation affects the morality of a proposed action. When pregnancy results from rape the description of the situation must take into account that such pregnancies are even more distressing than unwanted pregnancy following consensual intercourse. The consequences to both mother and child may be worse, if society refuses abortion to a woman, who has a deep, justified resentment at being forced to continue the pregnancy. The duty to follow a principle at cost is reduced, when the agent has not been responsible for the situation. A duty of care to a dependent human is less, when the duty was violently imposed. Certainly it is important to discover how situations arose, the past facts, but the past can be dealt with as part of the present.

An objection to forward moral thinking is that we all come to moral problems with individual moral baggage, our own worldview. My moral truth appals you. But the stepwise approach takes account of this relativism, because people's values are part of the process. It can take account of all moral systems. It encompasses utilitarianism but accepts the importance of moral principle. It takes account of feminine ethics, because it can recognise the importance of relationship and responsibility and try to balance those obligations against others. It can recognise general rights, specific obligations and personal goals. However different our worldviews are, we can start looking at a moral problem together.

15

When Is It Right To Kill Innocent Animals?

Can the suggested approach to moral problems help us to feel happier about choices we make with regard to killing other creatures?

- Is it right to kill and then eat other animals?
- Is it right to use them in medical experiments and then kill them?

EATING MEAT

As few of us hunt for our food we are talking about animals raised on farms, killed in abattoirs, butchered and sold to us in the supermarket.

Health facts

Our nearest relatives are the chimpanzees, and they kill monkeys and eat them when they can. Humans were always hunter-gatherers, eating animals and plants. Most of us became farmers 10,000 years ago and began to eat crops and livestock. So we have always been omnivores and are physiologically adapted to a mixed diet.

Vegetarians do not eat killed animals. They miss out on iron, high quality protein and omega-3 fatty acids, good for the heart and brain. Their diets may also be short in zinc, iodine, calcium, and Vitamin D. Iron is absorbed much better from meat than from plants. Adult men and older women do not need much iron in the diet but children do for growth and younger women do for menstruation, pregnancy, childbirth and lactation, which drain iron from them. Young vegetarian women are more likely to become anaemic than omnivores. Iron tablets would protect them but most of us are more likely to keep to an enjoyable, balanced diet than to take tablets regularly.

Vegans eat no animal products, not even eggs or milk, and this is difficult if you want to rely on natural products alone. They risk deficiency of vitamins A, D and B12; lack of vitamin B12 causes pernicious anaemia. These vitamins can be taken as manufactured tablets.

Children need protein to grow. Animal protein is better quality than vegetable protein because the amino-acids in it are more nearly in the right proportion for human needs. Because vegetarian diets are bulky children may not eat enough calories and protein.

The story is different for most adults. Vegetarians suffer less heart disease, less diabetes, less high blood pressure, fewer strokes and even less cancer than omnivores. A balanced vegetarian diet provides satisfactory nutrition. We eat too much red meat and dairy product in rich countries. Meat is too rich in saturated fat and cholesterol. Eating plenty of fruit and vegetables, as vegetarians do, is healthier.

Cruelty facts

Does eating animal products cause cruelty? It certainly can do. Some of the chickens we eat grow from hatchlings to table meat in a matter of weeks. That is more appropriate to growing a vegetable than to caring for a sentient creature. Their only blessing is that their lives are short.

In the UK all egg production is reasonably humane. Livestock are raised humanely but the journey to the abattoir is distressing. They may have a sense of impending doom as they wait near the slaughterhouse with the smell of death in their nostrils. The actual killing process is less important as unconsciousness supervenes very rapidly whether the animal is shot with a bolt or has its throat cut.

Other facts

We have to kill animals. Our dogs and cats are carnivores and pets are important to people. You can feed the children on muesli but not the dog. Guide dogs, sheepdogs, guard dogs, and sniffer dogs are all necessary. We poison the rats, which eat the grain, and the mice which invade our houses. They breed faster than you can trap them humanely. Still we do not have to kill as many animals.

Eating a lot of meat is selfish. Cattle contribute to global warming. The greenhouse gases, methane and carbon dioxide, produced by a cow equal that produced by a small car. It is more efficient to eat grain directly than to feed it to animals and then eat them. There would be more food for the growing population of the world if we ate less meat, although some land is suitable only for animal pasture.

Consequences

If we stopped eating meat we would reduce global warming and reduce cruelty to animals. Adults would be healthier. Food production would increase.

On the other hand we would put the health of children and young women at risk. We would deprive well-kept farm animals of a happy life. If we treat an animal well, we bring happiness into the world. Before considering principles the answer already seems to be to eat some animals but not as many.

Principles

Moral principles must be applied to raising animals to use as food. The objectives, which they indicate, must be assessed.

Non-maleficence. We should not cause unnecessary distress to any sentient creature. Cruelty to animals has been forbidden since biblical times.

The Lord opened the mouth of the ass and she said to Balaam "What have I done to thee that thou hast smitten me three times. Am I not thine ass, which thou hast ridden all thy life long? [Numbers 22.30]

Morality progresses even more erratically than science. Early and mediaeval Christian theology sometimes disregarded the interests of animals. Saint Augustine thought that animals did not exist in the same moral sphere as humans. Thomas Aquinas said: "It matters not how man behaves to animals; the apostle says God has no care of oxen". Fortunately many Christian saints loved animals, of whom the most celebrated is Saint Francis and modern Christianity takes a similar view.

Philosophers were no better. Descartes and Hobbes thought that animals were machines without feelings and their cries of distress were just reflexes. So some early experimenters nailed the paws of conscious dogs to boards to ensure their acquiescence to vivisection. Then they cut their vocal cords so that the cries of the animals did not disturb the peace of the laboratory.

Some early Christians were vegetarians from asceticism, not from regard for animals. They also abstained from sex and soap and called body lice the pearls of God. An hour after the murder of Saint Thomas Becket in Canterbury cathedral the lice all left him, valuing body warmth more than spiritual light. Cleanliness was not then next to godliness. This asceticism partly arose from the feeling that depriving oneself of brief physical pleasures in this world would bring permanent bliss in the next. It is like standing in the rain on Monday hoping it will make the sun shine on Tuesday.

We should avoid causing harm to humans. Devoting too much land to meat production increases global warming and reduces the calories available in the world.

Beneficence. We have a duty to ensure that the whole life experience of an animal in our care is good. In anthropomorphic terms its mother would want it to be born, even knowing what its fate would be. We must ensure that its life is better and its death is easier than it would be in nature, "red in tooth and claw". The livestock on a well-run farm have good lives. Anyone, who has watched a cockerel strutting happily with his harem of hens can see that. Certainly the cockerel has a good life.

> I was walking in the country with a friend, when we saw a sheep sleeping peacefully with its head on a rock. He said that it was a pity to kill the gentle creature to eat it. I replied that the good life it was having provided the justification for keeping it to kill it.

It is right to give animals a happy life. It is not morally obligatory to raise happy animals any more than it is to raise happy children. But it is very worthwhile to do so and domestic animals would not exist to enjoy good lives, if we did not use them. The more animals we provide with a good life, the more happiness we create. If they die painlessly at our hands rather than painfully at the hands of nature, that complements the good life we give them.

Giving children meat benefits their health. It is wrong for adults to deprive themselves of lawful pleasure. If the animal you eat had a good life, an easy death and was pastured on land unsuited to cereals, your conscience is clear.

Anti-speciesism. Treating animals differently from humans is speciesism and as wrong as racism and sexism. We are a different, not a superior creation. They have their lives and can suffer as we do. If it is wrong to do something to a human, then it is wrong to do it to a different animal.

This is a relevant principle but is it valid? Let us look at the practical implications. Is their suffering as important as human suffering? If a dog is in as much pain as a man, is its distress of equal importance? Clearly the comparison of pain suffered by two different species must be difficult, but it is the principle, which counts. According to this principle, if a man and a dog both have broken bones, but the nurse has only one dose of morphine, she should spin a coin to decide who gets it. Otherwise she is giving unfair preference to her own species.

Is the life of a horse as valuable as that of a human? It is true that humans usually live longer than horses, but the horse strives to live just as much as we do. Also parrots and giant tortoises can live longer than horses and that does not make their lives more valuable than the lives of horses. If humans do not come first, it would be wrong to throw a dog out of the last place in the lifeboat to accommodate a human. And if you are starving on a desert island with a boy and a dog, you should spin a coin to decide whether you and the boy should eat the dog or you and the dog should eat the boy. After all, dogs are more loyal and obedient than boys. And you may feel closer to a much-loved pet than to a strange boy. Perhaps a strict cannibal is more moral than a standard omnivore, because he at least eats only his own species. It all seems manifest nonsense. The natural response is that moral proximity must make us put humans first.

> Wisdom must go with sympathy, else the emotions will become maudlin and pity may be wasted on a poodle instead of a child – on a fieldmouse instead of a human soul. [1]

FEELING HAPPY AND MAKING HAPPY

However, what we have learned about animals quite recently lends a little weight to anti-speciesism. Activities, which we have regarded as confined to humans, are present in other animals in simple form, especially in apes. They strive for power, enjoy sex, want security and affection, kill other apes over territory, and value trust and co-operation. [2] Apes are self-aware, because they can recognise themselves in a mirror. They can plan ahead. A chimp gathered stones to throw at visitors later. They can fashion tools for a purpose and then use them successfully. Even crows can do that. Other primates also have culture, because they can learn a new skill and transmit it to succeeding generations. Japanese snow monkeys teach each other to wash sweet potatoes. Last and most important, apes may have a rudimentary moral sense. Other mammals such as elephants and dolphins share some of these features.

Anti-speciesism also has some religious sanction. Hindus think that cows should live out their natural lives. Jainism, an offshoot of Hinduism, insists on the absolute duty not to kill animals. Jain ladies will cover their mouths with cloths, in order not to swallow a fly, because it is fatal for the fly, not because it is unpleasant for the lady. Although if push came to shove, I suppose that they would sacrifice the fly for the lady.

Caring about the suffering of animals is morally obligatory. Accepting that they can have emotions and even a rudimentary moral sense is important. Treating them as moral equals is absurd.

> Humans have moral priority over other animals. I would think it morally outrageous, if someone preferred, faced with a choice, to save their dog rather than their even severely handicapped baby. It is the foundation of all morality. [3]

There are good reasons why human life is more valuable than other animal life. The death of a human causes distress to other humans. That affects animals to only a limited degree. The ewe suffers, when she loses her lamb but she soon forgets. Most animals do not recognise and love their adult offspring, whereas humans most emphatically do. Animals may suffer, when a stable companion is removed, but they neither know nor care that a former companion dies. The sheep does not grieve and go off its grass, when its half- sisters go to the abattoir. I am not pretending that there is an absolute distinction, with clear water between the different grief, which animals and humans feel on bereavement. Elephants and apes may suffer more like humans, but there is still a marked quantitative difference in the suffering. And I am not suggesting that we eat apes or elephants.

There are other morally significant differences between us and other animals. We have duties, purposes, plans and responsibilities. We respect each other's wish to fulfil them just as we want our own respected. A cow does not consider tomorrow, because it lives in the present. It has no moral responsibilities it wishes to undertake. It does not suckle its young out of duty but out of instinct. Animal pets give us great pleasure and they may be emotionally attached to us, but I doubt that they do anything for us out of a conscious sense of duty.

Then there is moral dilution. There is so much good to be done in the world but we can do only some of it. If you try to do good to all you finish by doing good to none. To give meaningfully to charity you have to select those which are dearer to you. If you are going to love donkeys as much as men, you will finish up loving men as little as donkeys. It is impossible to give practical love to all creatures great and small. A legacy to the cats' home means less for the orphanage. You cannot do everything or love everyone. If speciesism is wrong, where does care stop? Why are cuddly bunnies and cute dogs more morally important than rats? What about invertebrates? We can hardly concern ourselves about individual lobsters like individual humans, even though we want the species to survive. If we say that humans do not have moral priority, where do we draw the line?

Religious principles. The Judaeo-Christian ethic permits us to eat and exploit animals, avoiding cruelty. "At dusk ye shall eat flesh and in the morning ye shall be filled with bread." [Exodus 16.8] Clearly they already enjoyed toast for breakfast and steak for dinner. The bible rules out the full English breakfast, unless the hotel includes it in the room rate.

Jesus was neither a vegetarian nor an ascetic. He was a piscivore. He fed 5,000 people on fish. [Matthew 14.21] It is hardly likely that he told his disciples that fish was fine for the peasants, but personally he never touched the stuff. In the parable of the king's feast he talks quite uncritically of the butchery of cattle. [Matthew 22.4]

Choice

We have three main choices. Continue eating steaks galore; eat animal flesh occasionally and feed it more regularly to children; eat no animal products. Option one is good neither for us, nor for the hungry of this world nor for our planet. Option three puts children at risk and deprives many animals of a happy life but stops some cruelty.

Option two is the compromise and being moderate and English I like compromises. Life cannot run smoothly without them. The mother, who wants to feed her children well with limited funds, compromises. She buys animal protein pro-duced by factory farming, which is cheap but involves cruelty. She puts her children first. Vegetarians sometimes wear leath-er shoes because they find other materials uncomfortable. They find the cost of avoiding animal products too high and the cost of sticking to principles rigidly can be too high for any of us. Reasonable compromise is not hypocrisy.

MEDICAL RESEARCH

You eat meat but you will never experiment on animals. Nevertheless animal research is still a moral problem for you.

- Most of your doctor's knowledge is ultimately based on animal research.
- The drugs, which she gives you, have been tested on animals.
- It is hypocritical to benefit from the use of animals while claiming to oppose it. That would be like disapproving of burglary and receiving stolen goods.
- If animal experiments stop now, you personally will lose little, especially if you are older, because it takes many years for scientific advance to reach clinical practice. But our children and grandchildren will suffer.
- You are welcome to eschew medical help on moral grounds but not to deprive others of it.

The facts

How much cruelty is there to animals? There is not much because UK rules governing experiments are clear.

- All animal laboratories are registered and inspected.
- Repeated use of the same animal is forbidden.
- It is never permissible to inflict severe suffering. The experiment must be stopped and the animal destroyed, if that happens.
- The experiment must be scientifically sound and have some importance. Causing even mild distress or killing any creature is wrong, if it serves no useful purpose.

What animals are used? Advertisements depicting cute dogs are misleading. Most experimental subjects are rats, mice, and fish. Larger mammals figure in only 0.5% of experiments. Also it is illogical to worry more about the suffering of cute dogs and rabbits than the equal suffering of rats.

Is it necessary to use animals? Scientists do not experiment on live animals for pleasure. It is an expensive and inconvenient way of doing research and when there is any other way scientists turn to it. For example Salk, the American scientist, was able to make much faster progress in his work on polio vaccine, when he found that he could use cell cultures instead of live monkeys. Scientists are always trying to reduce the number of animals they use and replace animal experiments with other techniques, such as computer simulation and cell cultures. But these technologies cannot tell you what actually happens in the intact animal. If they could, nobody would use intact animals. A recent example of the failure of tests on human cell cultures to predict effects on intact humans was the disastrous injection of a monoclonal antibody into six volunteers. [4]

Thousands of candidate drugs are tested on animals and most of them discarded. It would be utterly irresponsible for anyone to subject a human to an entirely new chemical, be-fore trying it on another intact animal first, unless you value rats as highly as humans.

It is argued that humans have a unique physiology, dif-ferent from that of other animals. All mammals have a simi-lar physiology in many respects but each species differs from other species in some important respects. All individuals of the same species are very similar to other individuals but are also different in important ways. We do not each of us react to the same drug in the same way. Some benefit and some do not; the same drug, given for the same disease, cures some and kills others. You collapse and die after a penicillin injec-tion but I get better. The best way to predict the human re-sponse to a drug is to try it on other animals, and the best way to predict my response is to try it on other humans. But no test is perfect; there is no security this side of the grave; all life is probability.

> Thalidomide is often quoted as an example of the fail-ure of animal testing. It was introduced in 1957, as a sedative and remedy for the morning sickness of preg-nancy. However, it affected the blood supply to the de-veloping limbs of the foetus, and 15,000 babies were born with absent or vestigial limbs. It had been tested on pregnant rats, but unfortunately rats are very insen-sitive to the dangerous metabolites of the drug so it did not affect their babies. Also scientists then thought that drugs did not pass the placenta. But rabbits, mon-keys and humans are more sensitive to it. It was not a failure of animal testing; it was a disaster caused by in-sufficient animal testing. It was also a warning to avoid drugs as much as possible in early pregnancy. No ani-mal testing can give a total guarantee of safety.

Occasional disasters with new drugs will always occur. The longer a drug is in use and the more widely it is used the more the chance of discovering new problems. The newer the drug the more closely must it be monitored. Animal testing prevents most problems, not every problem.

> Starzl, the kidney transplant pioneer operated experimentally on four series of patients. Most patients in the first series died but most of the second group survived; nearly all the third group survived, as did the entire fourth group. The first three groups were dogs, and the fourth group were children.

Innovative surgery and equipment must also be tried first on animals. To operate on the heart it must be stopped. So a heart-lung machine or pump oxygenator is needed. In principle it is simple, but there are many problems to sort out in practice. Would you volunteer to go to certain death by being the first person to try out the prototype or would you depute that honour to a monkey?

We learn about diseases by studying animal models. A disease model may not be perfect but enormously useful information can be gained from it.

> In 1921 Banting and Best isolated insulin by tying off the pancreatic ducts of dogs. So the part of the pancreas producing digestive juices atrophied, and it no longer destroyed the insulin produced by the other part. They had to kill dozens of dogs before they succeeded. If they could not have experimented on live animals, years would have elapsed before insulin was discovered, and countless people would have died.

Consequences

It may be possible one day to eliminate the use of animals in medicine by computer simulation and cell culture, but that day is long in the future. If experiments on animals stopped some suffering would end, some animals would be deprived of overall satisfactory lives, and medicine would progress very much more slowly.

Experimentation on humans and other animals is a two way street. Animals suffer from the same physical and mental diseases as we do. Doctors and veterinarians work in allied professions and a doctor is just a vet, who knows how to treat only one species. What is learned from humans benefits other animals. About half the drugs used in humans are also used in animals. Investigations like radiology and surgical techniques are introduced for humans and then benefit other animals.

A British firm specialising in animal experiments allowed its standards to slip. It was driven out of the UK to the US by the illegal actions of animal rights activists, even though it had cleaned up its act. My experience in the US in 1968 was that experimental animals were treated very much worse there than in the UK. I saw turtles kept three deep in an inch of muddy water in a tin bath. What was done to them I will not describe. I hope they have also cleaned up their act. Those activists might have given a little thought to the consequences of their doings both for the animals and for the people, whose jobs they destroyed.

Principles and objectives

Non-maleficence. Cruelty is abhorrent. Animal lives are worthy of respect, even if they are not sacred, because they are living creatures like us and therefore as few as possible should be killed

Beneficence. There is a duty to benefit humans by all permissible means. The whole life principle demands that experimental animals be given good lives. We should provide them with a pleasant, not just a tolerable environment. They may currently be overfed, under exercised and bored. This should be remedied. Bored animals are stressed and this may vitiate experimental results. [5]. After they have been used they deserve whenever possible honourable retirement, not death.

Anti-speciesism. Insofar as animals are like us we should treat them like us. And insofar as they are different, we may treat them differently. We must ensure their happiness but there is no need to respect their autonomy.

Experiments on apes are not allowed in the UK but a small percentage of experiments involve monkeys. Because their brains are similar to our own they are especially important for neurological and psychological studies, for example into Parkinson's disease. But that means their minds are also more like ours and our moral proximity to them is greater. So the need to use them and concern about their use are both increased. Scrutiny of the experiments must be even stricter than with other animals. But in the last resort men are more important than monkeys.

Choice

It is right to benefit from research on animals, provided that as few as possible are used, serious cruelty is avoided, and their lives are overall happy.

16

Can It Be Right To Kill An Innocent Human?

Can it ever be right to kill a human, who wants to die, even if he has a good reason to want to die? And can it be right to kill the unborn life within a woman, even if she desperately wants it? Societies must decide whether to allow it. Doctors or others must decide whether to do it. Any of us may have to decide whether we want it done.

MERCY KILLING

An accountant enjoyed retirement for three years and then developed motor neurone disease. She tolerated the increasing incapacity with resignation but eventually she found the indignity it caused irksome. With no disrespect to her maker she wanted to give back her life. She felt that her story had been told. She was angry that her trusted family doctor refused to put an end to her unhappiness.

By euthanasia we mean killing someone to relieve his distress. By assisted suicide we mean helping someone to kill himself. They are not morally different and they shade into each other. It depends on how little or how much help a person needs to die. At one end of the spectrum a carer might "accidentally" leave a box of pills within reach of the patient. At the other end the carer gives a fatal injection on request to a disabled person. In between he provides a lethal drink.

Facts

Why should someone want to be killed, now that terminal care has improved so much? Pain can usually be controlled but some physical symptoms are harder to relieve. Also we hate the loss of dignity which occurs when increasing weakness stops us looking after our own bodily functions.

Killing is such a serious decision that it is especially important for both patient and carer to obtain the facts before making it. A palliative care specialist must confirm that it is impossible to reduce the sufferer's distress. A psychiatrist must ensure the absence of treatable, depressive illness. It is necessary to establish that the request is voluntary and sustained. A specially trained social worker might be the best person to ensure that termination of life is not requested out of guilt at being a burden or because of covert, unscrupulous pressure.

Consequences

On the one hand an unhappy, unwanted life comes to an end. On the other hand, if someone is killed, whose mind might have changed about it, a serious moral mistake has been made. Family may be pleased that the misery of a loved one has ended or distressed that death was deliberately hastened. If the practice becomes common, the general respect for human life may be diminished and some people might be wrongly killed. That needs further consideration.

Principles

Three moral principles are especially relevant to thinking about euthanasia: beneficence; respect for autonomy; respect for the sanctity of life.

Beneficence requires us to relieve distress. The issue is whether we may do so by helping a person to die. Some people need help to die because of physical incapacity. A medical prescription provides the easiest path to death. Death is a lonely journey, even if it ends in the arms of God, and the presence of someone loved and trusted is a comfort when we set out. Their presence also means that the action has been discussed and agreed with at least one person. So if and only if, it is right for a person to seek death, then it might be right to help him to do so. It is also better that it should be legal to help him. There are dangers in secrecy.

Respect for autonomy argues for compliance with a reasonable request but only with a reasonable request. However, there are extreme cases when the duty to relieve distress is so clear that it may outweigh even respect for autonomy. It can be right to kill someone without his permission, which is non-voluntary euthanasia.

In a film version of Fenimore Cooper's book *The Last of the Mohicans*, the hero, fleeing from the Indian camp, turns and shoots the British officer hanging screaming above the fire. [1] He does not ask his permission. How could he? How could he not kill him?

It can even be right to kill someone against his wishes, involuntary euthanasia.

The film *Lawrence of Arabia*, based on the book by T E Lawrence, *The Seven Pillars of Wisdom*, portrays his part in the Arab revolt against the Turks during the First World War. Lawrence leads a party of saboteurs to destroy a railway line and during the raid his devoted servant is badly injured. They cannot carry him with them and they believe that the Turks torture and kill prisoners. Lawrence takes out his pistol and shoots the young man, despite his pleas.

The argument in the first case is that the officer would have asked to be shot, if he could have conveyed his wishes. In the second situation Lawrence decided that the young man would later wish that he had been shot, if Lawrence had not shot him, a presumed retrospective consent. [2]

Respect for the sanctity of human life argues against suicide and assisting suicide. The examples above suggest that the duty of beneficence can trump both respect for the sanctity of life and respect for autonomy. There are no absolute principles and those who think that killing the innocent is absolutely forbidden, sometimes make exceptions in wartime.

The opposite view is that the duty to relieve distress, supported by respect for autonomy in all normal circumstances, sometimes outweighs the duty to preserve life. Morality is always situational and there are times when beneficence must prevail.

Choice

It seems so far that if someone desperately wants to die for good reason, it is right to help him. Sometimes the objective of relieving the distress of an individual human is so important that it outweighs other considerations. If your life is miserable and your death will distress no one, then it is not necessarily wrong to end your life. It follows that it can be right to help someone to die, if help is necessary. But there is a duty to consider carefully the effect of induced death on other people, on the family left behind, on the helpers and on society in general.

Other agents

Euthanasia involves more than a patient and his carer. It takes place in a society and involves family, friends, medical staff and legislators. They all have particular responsibilities, which must be considered. Legalising it might have an effect on future patients.

First I would say that we must be guarded about the views of two groups. Palliative care specialists claim that there is no need for mercy killing. To acknowledge that there was a need would imply a limitation to their skill. So they are interested parties. Bishops in Parliament offer reasons why legalisation would be mistaken but they would oppose it anyway on religious grounds. So their arguments might be disingenuous. However, we must always tackle the argument, not the person.

The doctor

Mercy killing, which does not involve a doctor is unsafe and so is such killing when a single doctor is involved.

> A doctor was prosecuted for stopping the heart of a distressed patient with a concentrated potassium injection. Intravenous injections of undiluted potassium can have only a lethal, not a therapeutic purpose. Potassium is always diluted in large infusion bottles. There was criticism that he should have taken further advice about pain control.

Using death as a means of treatment has always been illegal and still is in most countries. Let us look at the duties of a doctor to decide whether mercy killing could be one for those prepared to be involved. A doctor's prime function is to preserve and restore normality, as far as possible. She should be guided by the duty of beneficence controlled by respect for autonomy. More specifically her duties are as follows.

- She should prevent and relieve distress and disability and prolong life.
- She should achieve the goals in the most efficient way acceptable to the patient.
- She should accept the priority assigned to those goals by the rational patient, when they conflict with each other or with non-medical aspirations.

- The needs of other patients may limit her effort for the individual.
- Her conscience may limit her options, in which case she should refer the request to another doctor.
- She has a duty to obey the law. It is dangerous to claim that conscience puts one above laws voted by an elected assembly. Illegal actions cannot be openly discussed as such a serious matter should be. Legalisation would deal with that problem but until it does doctors must be wary of mercy killing.

Recently doctors have legally undertaken other activities unrelated to a quest for normality.

- They use surgery to make people look younger than they are.
- They help healthy people of both sexes have sex without the risk of pregnancy.
- They kill foetuses in the interest of the foetus, because it is likely to have an unhappy life because of disability.
- In many jurisdictions they kill foetuses in the interest of a potential mother.

The issue is whether they should further extend their role to mercy killing and use killing humans after birth as a therapeutic tool. They have never done so, at least not openly. It would be a strange departure from their traditional role. Might it make some patients fear non-voluntary euthanasia? The answer to that problem is that termination of life should be the province of those specially trained to do it, not the doctor, who looks after the patient. It is for her to guard the patient against unjustified killing. Perhaps retired doctors, nearer to needing it, should do it?

The legislator

Although mercy killing remains illegal in the UK, prosecutions have largely ceased. Should legislators change the law? Their duty is to protect citizens and therefore decide whether legalisation would do more harm than good overall. But even in a secular democracy law should also reflect the collective moral view. There are arguments which favour legalising assisted suicide.

- Illegality hinders prior consultation.
- It promotes disrespect for the law, because the law does not stop it.
- A citizen is harmed when a reasonable request for life termination is refused. There is security in knowing that our lives will go on only as long as we want them to. Choice is an important benefit.
- The "general will" in the UK has swung round to favour legal assisted suicide.

There are also reasons why legalisation might not serve the public.

- We have an excellent palliative care resource in the UK. More good may come from further improving palliative care than from legalising mercy killing. Doing so might remove some of the pressure to improve palliative care.

- However careful the precautions, dying people may opt for assisted suicide because they feel a burden to others, not because they really want it. Others may privately encourage them to opt for it.
- There is a slippery slope problem. People will always test the limits of what the law allows.

Experience in other countries suggests that the slippery slope is the main problem. The extension of mercy killing to those not dying is a danger. Some younger people suffering from severe permanent disability, for example tetraplegia, will opt for it. Many will find life in that situation rewarding despite their physical problems; some will find it intolerable despite prolonged rehabilitation. Their distress is caused by a medical problem so perhaps a medical solution is permissible.

There are also those whose lives are utterly bleak, even though they have no illness or disability. Perhaps they have lost all their family. I have sympathy with their wish to die but medicine should not be used to solve problems which are not medical. There must always be a restraining fence on a slippery slope. It is possible to manage the dangers, which legalising euthanasia, will cause. [3]

Non-voluntary killing may be proposed for those, whose life has no positive quality, such as the severely demented.

I was asked to see a severely demented man because of an abnormality in a blood test. I was unnerved when I entered a room of about twenty such unfortunate adults in diapers, some uttering cries, some rocking back and forward, and some banging their heads. The staff deserved the utmost respect. It was a humbling experience.

Intuitively the idea of killing these humans appals us. Repugnance is a warning, not a prohibition but here it has reasoned justification. These humans would be killed in the interests of the State, not in their own interest. That is what the Nazis did and it is sensible to refuse to start down a path which has led others to depravity. The quality of their lives could be somewhat improved. If we can afford so many ridiculous luxuries, we should pay whatever is necessary to do that. It would probably mean employing more staff. A second objection is the absence of informed consent. A third objection is that killing them would be a betrayal of the carer's duty. The fence on this particular slippery slope is the rule that all humans must be treated as ends in themselves.

ABORTION

Analogies can help us examine our moral dilemmas. When we do not know what to do we find a similar situation, where we have a firm intuition about what to do. We isolate the principle underlying the intuition and apply it to the new situation. The Common Law uses a similar idea when deciding what to do in the present case by seeing what was done in previous cases. A famous article used the following analogy to downplay the duty to continue a pregnancy at cost. [4]

> A great musician has a fatal kidney disease, from which he would recover, if he could be kept alive for six months. While you are asleep the society of music lovers attaches your circulation to his to keep him alive. Are you morally obliged to maintain the connection for six months, to your great inconvenience or could you disconnect yourself and let him die?

The author concludes that it would be worthy to maintain the connection but not obligatory, and by implication it is worthy to endure an unwanted pregnancy but not obligatory. But the situations are different in important respects. Carrying a pregnancy is not physically the same as walking around tied by a tube to another adult. You are not genetically related to the musician but you are to the foetus, which increases the duty to it. Also it can only be compared to pregnancy resulting from rape but most unwanted pregnancies follow consensual intercourse. If you take the risk, you have a duty to accept the consequence. Someone else could volunteer her own circulation to the composer and let you off the hook or the tubing so responsibility is shared. No one can volunteer her womb in place of yours. Is the life of a foetus as important as that of an adult? Is passively withdrawing support necessary to life the same as active killing? Are the prospects for the musician and the foetus similar?

Like many analogies it instructs by its failure. Situations are rarely identical. But analogies can clarify thought about the facts of a situation and feed into the four-step process.

Facts

To make the right decision about an abortion a woman needs the facts. She has to take account of the maturity of the foetus, its post-natal prospects, and sometimes its normality. She must consider her physical and mental health and her social situation. She must think about her other children and her emotional and moral attitudes to abortion. She may want facts and opinions from doctors and counsellors.

Consequences

The woman's two possible actions are killing the foetus or carrying it to term. It is necessary to make the best possible prediction about the effect of either course on her physical and mental health and the moral distress, which abortion might cause her. If in her heart she thinks abortion is wrong, she may suffer later distress. We must consider the likely fate of the baby if she proceeds with the pregnancy. If she has other children it is necessary to consider the effect of another child on their welfare.

Principles

Respect for the sanctity of life is again a central issue. Does the scope of that principle extend fully to prenatal humans from the time of conception?

In only a few countries is voluntary euthanasia permissible but abortion is legal in many more. It seems strange that it should be legal to kill a healthy human, neither asking to die nor having any reason to do so, but illegal to kill a dying human, asking to die with good reason. This paradox has two possible, related explanations. Insofar as the function of law is predominantly the protection of citizens it means that we do not regard foetuses as full citizens. Insofar as law is a distorted reflection of public morality it suggests that we ascribe less moral importance to a human before it is born than after.

Age is not relevant to the sanctity of life after we are born; it is as wrong to kill an old man as a young man. Is it also irrelevant before we are born? Is it just as wrong to kill a prenatal human, when it is one cell, as after it has grown to be a baby ready to be born? Are prenatal humans morally important for what they currently are or for what they will be, their potential.

The process of development is gradual and continuous, but there are incremental points. We all start as a single cell, a fertilised egg. Then the embryo of a few cells fixes to the wall of the uterus. Next the primitive streak appears at about two weeks; it becomes the single, individual human. After four weeks the heart starts to beat. At about 26 weeks the peripheral nerves connect to the brain, and the foetus becomes sentient, if not conscious. At about this time with modern medical care it can live separate from the body of the mother. Birth is a gigantic physiological milestone, which has always been of legal importance, and which is likely to be of moral importance. The human can no longer rely on his mother to supply him with warmth, oxygen, and food, and carry away his waste products. He must perform these functions for himself or can rely on strangers to help him. The moral status of the human probably changes at these incremental points.

Certainly the potential of an entity must affect our treatment of it. We do not plant acorns in the flowerbed. A human embryo is morally different from a cat embryo. You treat a child as a child but with awareness that it will become an adult, and what you do to it in childhood will affect what it becomes as an adult. If you do not kill the foetus, it will probably one day have the capacity to plan, enjoy life, and undertake the responsibilities and enjoy the pleasures which fall to rational humans. Therefore there is a duty not to kill any developing human, even a fertilised egg.

Arguments dismissing the importance of potential are weak. The embryo may split spontaneously to form two humans. That makes it more important. It may fuse with another embryo to form a chimera but that is so rare that it can be disregarded. Many embryos do not implant and some that do die early. But it is not right to kill someone because he might die anyway. Some ridicule the importance of potential by pointing out that the sperm before it enters the egg and the egg, before the sperm enters it, are jointly a potential human. Dozens of eggs and millions of sperm cannot all be sacred. However, the paint and the canvas do not make a painting until the artist starts to put them together with an idea in mind. Only when the egg is fertilised does it become a potential, individual person.

Accepting that potential is morally important, is it all-important? Actuality is also important. A fertilised egg does not have the same moral value as a baby about to be born. An acorn is not an oak tree and we cannot swing from its branches. We do not treat the child as the adult it will become. Parents grieve more at the loss of an eight-month pregnancy than at the loss of a six-week embryo. [5] As the embryo matures the probability of the birth of a healthy baby increases. How can something no bigger than a pinpoint be as important as the healthy baby, which the mother is about to deliver?

The conclusion must be that a human has moral importance as soon as the egg is fertilised. But its moral importance increases as it develops and so must the duty to respect its life.

Beneficence

The mother may abort her foetus to benefit it, if it will live for only a few years, and rather miserably at that. Prolonging a life of suffering is wrong but it is not simply a matter of refraining from treatment, because it is necessary to kill it. Abortion becomes prenatal euthanasia.

There is also a slippery slope problem. If it is right to kill a very defective foetus, then why is it wrong to kill a less severely defective foetus?

Abortion was sought for a child with a cleft palate, and a charming young woman priest, born with a cleft palate, very understandably opposed it.

No rule can be given. After full discussion of the situation the pregnant woman herself must decide whether she can give the foetus in her body a reasonable chance of reasonable happiness.

A woman may seek the abortion even of a healthy foetus in the interest of her existing children. If they need their mother, she would be downright wrong not to save her life by abortion. If they need her strength, and cannot afford to dilute their share of food, she would be wrong not to abort. If she is already having difficulty feeding and educating seven children, then she has no business producing an eighth. But it is silly saying that the woman should not have sex, because often she has no choice. What is the point of telling her to use contraception, if it is not available? The situation is analogous to that of the man, who steals bread to feed his children. There are situations where it is less evil to do active wrong, than to do passive wrong by failing in a duty of care.

I am not forgetting that a disabled child may have a happy life, be a blessing to the family, a focus of love, and an opportunity for moral growth in all members of the family. Morality is situational. Only individuals can make difficult, personal decisions, because only they know what they are and how they are placed.

Respect for autonomy

A foetus has no wishes, so the duty is to act in its best interest. But many think that a woman is entitled to do what she wishes with her own body. People talk of a woman's right to choose. It is a claim that all abortion should be legal; it cannot be a claim that all abortion is moral. We have a legal right to adultery but not a moral right to indulge in it.

Cost

The cost to a woman of continuing a pregnancy is a continuous spectrum. Abortion to save one's life is morally obligatory; abortion for the sake of a holiday is wicked. The more mature the foetus, the higher must be the cost of preserving its life to justify killing it. Thus intrauterine devices prevent early embryos implanting in the uterus, effectively killing them. Two factors weaken the duty to preserve their lives. The first is immaturity. They are still only a few cells. The second is that the woman has little moral proximity to them, as she does not know that they exist. Turn to the other extreme. We have a twenty-week foetus and abortion can be justified only by severe danger to the mother's health. The decision is made on a case-by-case basis and no text can offer rules.

Of course abortion has a cost in sadness and guilt but it is for the mother to decide whether continuation or termination of the pregnancy will be more costly.

People say they would never do something. It is often because they cannot imagine themselves in a situation, in which they would have to pay the cost of not doing it. When the unexpected happens to them, they may find very good excuses for doing it, applicable only to themselves. I heard an American abortionist on the radio say that women, who demonstrated regularly outside her clinic, occasionally came in for an abortion. They even returned to the picket line afterwards. We are good at dividing our minds into compartments.

The choice

It is wrong to deny that the moral arguments about abortion are powerful each way. Extreme views risk being blind or hypocritical. It is wrong to beg this serious moral question by the emotive use of language. Before eight weeks of maturity the developing human is correctly called an embryo and after that it is a foetus. At six months or so it becomes an unborn baby. That does not make it right to destroy any human life without good reason.

Abortion is a continuous, quantitative moral spectrum, not a simple qualitative choice, except for the extremist. The maturity of the foetus, its possible disabilities, and the cost of continuing the pregnancy to the mother and her family are continuous variables. That makes the decision difficult and individual.

Morality is always situational. The passionate supporter of the woman's right to choose should be appalled at the destruction of human life for trivial reasons. The most committed anti-abortionist must surely admit that abortion is justified to save a woman's life. In the wide territory in between it is for the individual conscience to decide.

Other people's duties

The doctor, who thinks abortions are immoral, has the right to refuse any involvement in them. But she must inform all potential patients of her attitude so that they know to go elsewhere. Delaying an abortion harms the woman and increases the immorality of the killing, once you accept that the moral status of the foetus increases during pregnancy. A doctor should not use a position of power to impose a personal morality on another rational adult. But because she is trying to protect a third human she may, as one equal to another, put the negative side of abortion.

The earlier a pregnancy is terminated the less the State need be involved and the more it is a matter of personal morality. Emergency contraception works before the woman even knows she is pregnant. Medical abortions before six weeks of pregnancy are simpler than surgical abortions, which involve doctors, nurses, and clinics. In those situations the State is unavoidably involved and has a duty to regulate the process. Abortion ceases to be a purely personal matter.

Society is obliged to supervise the actions of health care workers and clinics. The law should forbid them to act in ways which are generally regarded as evil. In the UK there is no overwhelming moral objection to early abortion and in the US opinion is divided. The law should prohibit actions which harm society. If abortion harmed society prohibition would be justified. But few countries are in desperate need of unwanted babies. Women denied safe, legal abortion often undergo unsafe, illegal abortion. That costs the country more.

The law should protect citizens. In UK law we are not legal entities for many purposes until we are born. As soon as a human emerges into our world, naked, defenceless and bawling we recognise it as a citizen, with all the rights to protection of a citizen. From then on the State tries to protect us both from deliberate harm even by our mothers and from deliberate neglect by those, who owe us a duty of care. The issue is how far back before birth the public duty to us should extend. The most widely accepted answer is back to the point, at which we are unlikely to develop into moderately happy citizens, if separated from our mother's body. At the moment in the UK we set that point at 24 weeks gestation. It follows that abortion should be legal by personal consent up to that point. After that society rightly has an input into the decision.

Conclusion

We want to do the best with the life we have, whether or not another one awaits us. When we look back on our lives we want to think that we have been as happy as our characters and our circumstances have allowed.

We want to feel that we have made a modest contribution to the happiness of others. We care most about those nearest to us, such as our children, but we also have some care for the happiness of those who have crossed our path. We should try to follow moral principles but we must always hope that doing so will promote the happiness of those around us.

To be happy is a benefit to us and a duty to others. Happy people are more inclined to make others happy and that in turn makes them happier. Laughter epitomises this. It is a very human activity and when we laugh with others our pleasure is greater than when we laugh alone.

Some of us are born with a sunny disposition, which makes us feel happy and enjoy the happiness of others. Even when we are not so lucky we can try to do something about it. This book offers some advice about what to do. I hope you found my thoughts interesting, sometimes amusing and occasionally useful.

References And Notes

Chapter 1 What is happiness?
1. Kant I. *Groundwork for the Metaphysics of Morals.* Section 1; "I am never to act otherwise than so that I could also will that my maxim should become a universal law."
2. Kant I. *Critique of Practical reason.*
3. Fowler J H, Christakis N A. *Dynamic Spread of Happiness,* BMJ 2008;337: 2338.
4. Janosi M. *Personal communication.*

Chapter 2 How do we find happiness?
1. Goethe J W. (1749-1831) Goethe's Gespraeche, In Gollancz V. *A Year of Grace* Penguin 1955, 126.
2. Mark 11: 15-17.
3. Compare. "The psalmist tells us to leave off evil and then do good. If you find it difficult, you may first do good and evil will automatically leave you." Yitzhak Meir, second century, In Golllancz See 1,126.
4. Abba Arika (160-247) in See 3.
5. Aristotle *Nichomachean Ethics.*
6. At the time Huxley wrote a strange theory was current - that humans were apes born before full foetal development.
7. Wolfe W B. Cit. Jarski R. *A Word from the Wise.* Ebury Press, 2006.

8. Milton J. *On His Blindness* (Sonnet).

Chapter 3 Why happiness is the ultimate good

1. Kant I. *Critique of Practical Reason*, Conclusion.

2. Mill J S *Utilitarianism*, Chapter 1. Penguin Books, London 1977, 93.

3. Glover J. *Causing Death and Saving Lives*. Penguin 1977.

4. Thomas D. *Under Milk Wood*.

5. Kant I. *Grounding for the Metaphysics of Morals*, Section 1.

Chapter 4 Growing old and staying happy.

1. Marvell A. *To his coy mistress,* (poem).

2. Declaration on Euthanasia. *Sacred Congregation for the declaration of the Faith*. Vatican City, 1908, 6-11.

Chapter 5 Feeling more peaceful about dying.

1. Epicurus. (341-271BC) *Letter to Menoeceus.*

2. Shakespeare W. *Hamlet,* Act 3, Scene 1.

3. Marlowe C. *The Tragical History of Doctor Faustus.*

Chapter 6 Justice between the Generations.

1. Kennedy JF. *Special message to the Congress on the needs of the nation's senior citizens*. February21,1963.

2. BMJ 2011, 342, 402.

3. Journal of the Royal College of Physicians, London. June/July1995.

4. Mitchell, S C M et al. *Age and Ageing* 1993,22, 443-9.

Chapter 7 Why does making other people happy make us happy?

1. Forster M. *Hidden Lives* Penguin 1995.

2. Hamzelou J. *New Scientist* 09/10/2010,14.

3. Darwin C. (1809-82) *The Expression of the Emotions*.

4. Barash D. in Singer P. ed. *Ethics*, Oxford University Press 1994, 63.

5. Paul, Romans 7:15.

6. In Latin *Video meliora proboque, deteriora sequor*.

Chapter 8 Our happiness or their happiness?

1. Leibniz G. *Discourse on Metaphysics*, 34.

2. Blake W. *Jerusalem* 55,1,60.

3. Plato. (427-347BC)*The Republic*, book 7.

4. Axel Oxenstierna (1583-1654) renowned Swedish chancellor in a letter to his son in 1648.

Chapter 9 Reasons to care about the happiness of others

1. Hume D. *An Enquiry Concerning Human Understanding*, section 10.

2. Spinoza B. *Ethics* part 2, appendix.

3. She also sang with her handsome Toni: "There's a place for us, a time and place for us." She was wrong. We can have no time but the present.

4. Hume D. *Dialogues Concerning Natural Religion*.

5. Johann Scheffler aka Angelus Silesius (1624-77) German physician and poet In Gollancz See C2:1, 315.

6. Exodus 10, 27. There was no need for the Egyptians to suffer so much, as God could have softened, not hardened Pharaoh's heart.

7. Jones D. *New Scientist* 2005 26/11, 34.

8. Aristotle *Nichomachean ethics.*

9. Huxley J. *Essays of a Humanist*, Penguin 1966, 222.

10. Huxley J. as 10

Chapter10 Should we really care about the happiness of others?

1. Hobbes D. *Leviathan*, Chapter14.
2. Aristotle. *Nichomachean Ethics*, Book 1.
3. Nietszche F. *Beyond Good and Evil*, Chapter 7.
4. Pence G. Virtue Theory in Singer P. ed. *A Companion to Ethics*, Blackwell 1991.
5. Wood M. *Conquistadors*. BBC Worldwide, London 2000, 160.
6. Wood M. as above, 259-260.

Chapter 11 How should we go about making others happy?

1. "Can" does not imply "ought" but "ought" implies aware and "can." I have to hear your cries and have access to a lifebelt.
2. Kant I. *Metaphysics of Morals*.
3. Matthew 7:12.
4. Confucius. Analects In Singer P. *Ethics*. Oxford University Press, 76.
5. Adler A. In Jarski R. *A Word from the Wise*. Ebury Press 2006, 211.
6. Rothschild W. *Personal communication*.
7. Grahame Greene In See 5, 510.
8. The principle is based on Paul, Romans 3, 8. "Why not say then: 'Let us do evil so that good may come'? Some people have insulted me by accusing me of saying this very thing."
9. after Glover J.

Chapter 12 Religious duty or general happiness?

1. Dryden J. *The Hind and the Panther* (poem).
2. Marx K. *Critique of Hegel's Philosophy of Right*, 1843, Introduction.

3. Bunam of Pzhysha Hasidic rabbi d.1827 In Gollancz See C 2:1, 8. Haisidism is a mystical Jewish sect, which emphasises joy in divine worship.

4. Hume D. *Dialogues concerning natural religion*, Chapter 12.

5. Angelus Silesius See C2:1, 315.

6. Augustine (354-430) *Confessions*, Book 11.

7. Huxley J. *Religion without revelation*.

8. Weinberg S in Dawkins R. *The God Delusion* Transworld Publishers 2007, 283.

9. Buber M. *Tales of the Hasidim*: early masters. Schocken paperbacks 1947, 100.

10. Dawkins R See 8, 349-54.

11. Milgram S. *Behavioral study of obedience*, 1963.

Chapter 13 Tackling decisions

1. Campbell A.

1. Singer P. All animals are equal. In Singer P. ed. *Applied Ethics*. Oxford University Press 1986, 215-228.

Chapter 14 Making decisions

1. Savulescu J. *Journal of medical ethics*.

2. See C11, 3.

3. Singer P. *Writings on an ethical life*. Harper Collins 2000, 287.

4. Grimshaw G. The idea of a female ethic. In Singer P. ed. *A companion to ethics* Blackwell 1993, 491-9.

5. Beauchamp T L. The four-principles approach. In Gillon R ed. *Health care ethics*. John Wiley 1994, 9-11.

Chapter 15 When is it right to kill innocent animals?

1. Warnock M. *An Intelligent Person's Guide to Ethics*, Duckworth, London 1998.

2. De Waal F. *Primates and Philosophers*, Princeton University Press 2006.

3. see1. 68-9

4. Mayor S. *British Medical Journal* 332,683. Nor did animal tests predict the disaster.

5. Durham D. Bored to Distraction. *New Scientist*, 10/12/2009, 26.

Chapter 16 Can it be right to kill an innocent human?

1. Fenimore Cooper, 1826.

2. Actually in the book he resigns himself to being shot but a book and the film based on it are two different works of art. Fiction can make valid moral points.

3. Bernheim J. et al. Development of palliative care and legalisation of euthanasia: antagonism or synergy? *British Medical Journal*, 2008,336, 864-7.

4. Thomson J.J. A defence of abortion. *Philosophy and Public Affairs* 1:1(Fall 1971), 47-76.

5. Dworkin R. *Life's Dominion* HarperCollins; 1993, 86-7.

Printed in Great Britain
by Amazon.co.uk, Ltd.,
Marston Gate.